Designed and executed by Lieut Colonel Graham Seton Hutchison D.S.O., M.C., F.R.G.S. 1935.

Name...

Regiment..

Rank ....

Service...

....

....

....

Works by the same Author

THE THINKER ON THE BUTTE DE WARLENCOURT

Sir William Orpen, R.A.

PILGRIMAGE

BY

LT.-COL. GRAHAM SETON HUTCHISON

D.S.O., M.C., F.R.G.S.

LONDON
RICH & COWAN, LTD.
25 SOHO SQUARE, W.1

First published November 1935
Reprinted . . August 1936

MADE IN GREAT BRITAIN

PRINTED AND BOUND BY RICHARD CLAY AND SONS, LIMITED, BUNGAY, SUFFOLK,
FOR MESSRS. RICH AND COWAN, LIMITED, 25 SOHO SQUARE, LONDON, W.1

To Mark the Unique Occasion of the Unveiling
of the Canadian War Memorial on Vimy Ridge

BY

HIS MAJESTY KING EDWARD VIII

26TH JULY 1936

And as a slight signal of respectful devotion to
the memory of fallen Canadians in the Great
War 1914–1918

THIS VOLUME,

dedicated by gracious permission to the Sovereign,
whose comradeship towards the men with whom
he served in the field has never failed,

IS PRESENTED

to the Veterans who participated in the Pilgrimage
to the former Battlefields in gratitude for the
Services to the land which the donor long since
learned to love

BY

LORD QUEENBOROUGH, G.B.E.

Canfield Place,
Hatfield.

CONTENTS

CONTENTS

ILLUSTRATIONS

INTRODUCTION

THE PILGRIM TRAVELS

Spirit of pilgrimage—Design of the book—How to travel—Tours planned—How to use the book.

THE pilgrim is one who travels, usually far and in a strange land, to visit some holy place. And a pilgrimage is a journey to a shrine, or to some place of association regarded as sacred. The men who journeyed to France and Flanders to fight the battles of the nations were pilgrims indeed, for all human life may be regarded as a journey, especially, as Shakespeare wrote, as one to a future blessed state. The fields of Flanders and of Picardy are everywhere filled with memories of those who journeyed thus. And the pilgrim who revisits the scenes of his former pilgrimage, or those who visit them for the first time, must be very conscious of an impression that this ground for ever will be sacred.

A pilgrim may travel alone, or in company with his wife and children, or in that of his closest and dearest friends. And this last undoubtedly is the best way in which to undertake any pilgrimage or to fill the leisure hours. He may travel on foot, when, though he may not see so much, he will feel more. He may journey by bicycle, or be borne swiftly over the roads by motor-car. To visit one battlefield or to see a single cemetery, the pilgrim will be well advised to travel mostly on foot, because then the impression will be the more enduring, for he can keep his vigil as he will. But if, as is more probable, the pilgrim desires to revisit many scenes or to obtain a full and fair view of the battlefields and of the memorials which stand thereon, since time is limited and circumstance is usually the arbiter of behaviour, he must travel by motor-car, and usually as one of a large party. He may and should be filled with gladness, for each village recalls many scenes of youthful frolic and fun, though the fields and woods around may have been darkened by deep tragedy. The pilgrim should remember that for many Calvary was the greatest tragedy of all history, but without it there was no promise of the Eternal. So, though he treads upon sacred ground, he must not permit any morbid sense to overcome that gladness and pride in sacrifice which is all the dead themselves would have desired to their memory.

In their tour many pilgrims pause and stand sometimes in meditation, reflecting upon the deeds of valour, so many of them untold, and of sacrifice that will never be known, of which the landscape has been the witness and that nearly every village knew.

Except in their topographical outline, the battle-fields have changed. The rebuilded towns and villages and the resown fields, yielding their crops, bear no resemblance to the crumbling ruins, shattered woods and shell-pitted wastes which marked the War years. And for the pilgrim, revisiting the scene, it may even be difficult to rediscover villages and scenes whose every stone and contour in former years were as familiar as the palm of the hand. But the pilgrim will find that by night the old instinct will reassert itself, and, blind in the darkness, he will be able to walk with certainty to any one of the old familiar spots. But since the pilgrim goes to see and to re-experience and not to grope in darkness, this book will assist him to move freely ; to enlighten ; to find what he seeks ; and to be possessed of that essential knowledge without which he cannot picture the battlefields and re-people the towns and villages with the soldiers of the nations.

The purpose of this volume is to provide the pilgrim of the battlefields with the story of their great events. Further, through this book those who sit at home will be possessed of a storehouse of knowledge concerning British feats of arms, and from its pages will be able to picture the life and death of those who gave everything that a higher civilization and understanding between peoples might evolve.

The pilgrim, with this volume, can follow the course of events from the beginning to the end. He can make a study of one district, of one battle-field, even of a village. He will learn to understand the character of the inhabitants, and their history. He will obtain a view of the association between landmarks and those varied races, on one side or the other, who strove together for their possession. Before visiting any scene, he can equip himself with knowledge, so that the undulating downs, the copses and the villages become peopled again by soldiers, enduring untold hardship, or playing to-gether in an enduring comradeship. The rise and fall of ground will obtain their true significance. The great events of the War are laid bare. The whole history of Flanders, of Picardy, of North-eastern France, rich in historical association, for British, French and Germans alike, is opened.

Throughout these pages, from personal narrative, also, are presented cameos of the greatest events or of typical experience with which each battlefield is associated. There are four such eye-witness accounts.

The book is divided, for convenience, into chapters, limited to separate areas; and for the most part, such limits fix time as well as place.

As the War years recede, visits to the battlefields are becoming not less rare, but are increasing. There are literally thousands of histories of the Great War. This book provides a synthesis. It is not intended to be a history, nor does it enter into strategic and tactical controversy, for it is concerned with events as and where they happened.

The book is written primarily for the pilgrim. It is intended also for the Public Library of every town and village, whose territorial associations with Flanders and with Picardy are linked for ever by the battlefields and established through the Memorials and Cemeteries.

The chapters are arranged in accordance with the magnitude of effort and of event. It might have been convenient to number these from North to South. But it will be observed that the highest interest throughout the Great War is to be found in Picardy. Not only were the most important battles fought in this area, but it is one also whose beauty has long been recognized, while its historical associations are buried deep in British history. It will be found, also, that, as in a campaign, a base is necessary to the traveller and visitor. For the Somme battles, Amiens provides such a point, from which extends in fan shape the whole battlefield.

Ypres is the base for the Salient. Cassel or Haze-brouck for the Battle of the Lys : Arras or St. Pol for the Battle of Arras. Each separate battlefield is considered, therefore, as a fan ; and it will be found that the National Roads lead eastwards from the points named, convenient to the exploration of the battlefields as a whole, or for the purpose of visiting one sector, a Memorial or a Cemetery. In designing the book, therefore, what was found convenient and necessary during the War has been followed for the advantage of traveller and reader.

As the chapters are divided into the regions of the great battles, so, also, the Itinerary for the pilgrim corresponds with the method employed in laying out this book. The pilgrim must have his base. He will find, whether travelling by himself or with a party, that the National Roads, linking one town with another and interlacing the battlefields, are conveniently served by regular services of public motor conveyances. Travel is cheap. The traveller can move from one point to another with comparative ease ; and in every town and in almost every village he will find good hostelry for the night and every-where and at any time a warm welcome and a good meal.

In making a recommendation to the traveller, the beauty of much of the landscape and the historical interest of many of the towns of Flanders and of Picardy should be emphasized. Through centuries, Flanders and Picardy have served as the inspiration for poets and painters ; and amid these scenes some of the greatest names among them have produced the world's masterpieces. So that, though primarily

B

perhaps in these days the area of the battlefields may be regarded as ground sacred with memory, it is also rich in its landscape, fair of face, and a truly wonderful pleasure ground for man in his leisure hours.

Two battlefields are of the highest interest, namely those of the Somme and of Ypres. That of the Somme is vast in extent; and, if all is to be seen, three days at least should be devoted to the area; while that of the Ypres Salient can be covered in two days, though such a visit would not do the Salient full justice.

The base from which to visit the Somme battlefield is Amiens, an important railway centre and easily accessible within a few hours from Calais, Boulogne or Paris. There are two or three good hotels, but several other inns and hostelries serve the tourist, whose hospitality and impeccable cleanliness provide all that could possibly be desired.

Four main roads go east from Amiens. First, that to Albert, from whence omnibus services continue north-east to Bapaume or due east through Mametz, Curlu and Cléry to Péronne. Second is the road, so much used by marching troops during the War, which, following the course of the River Somme, travels due east through Corbie to Bray and thence to Péronne. The third road, also going due east, lies south of the Somme and is serviced by motor-buses: it proceeds through Villers Bretonneux to Villers Carbonnel, where is an important road junction, leading north to Péronne and south to Roye. The main road continues to St. Quentin, and is that which should be taken to view the battlefields of August, 1914, and of September to November, 1918.

Farther south is the fourth road, with Montdidier on its right, leading to Roye. In order to view the ground covered by the First Battle of the Somme, it is recommended that the traveller should first proceed to Albert, passing Querrieu. He may then turn south to Bray, crossing the ridge between the River Ancre and the Somme, from the summit of which extends the panorama of the Albert battlefield. He should then proceed through Cappy and Flacourt, across an area which for many months was completely devastated, until he reaches Péronne. From this town the southern route may be taken to Villers Carbonnel, and thence following the line of the main German advance in March, 1918, to Villers Bretonneux, where stands a stone marking the limit of the German advance. This route, covering sixty-five miles, can be followed by private charabanc or motor-car.

But this tour omits a visit to the area of High Wood and the Flers Ridge, which for so long was the most keenly contested point of the whole battlefield. From Albert, therefore, the journey may well be extended along the Bapaume road to Courcelette. At the road corner is the friendly Marquant Café, a hospitable halting-place. The traveller then takes the road to the right, through Martinpuich, carrying on to High Wood, from which a superb panorama is obtained over all points of the compass. He proceeds towards Longueval; and then through Guillemont and Curlu to Péronne; or by an alternative route through Ginchy and Combles to the same destination. The traveller can then elect to return to Amiens through Cappy, Bray, Morlancourt and Corbie. There is no doubt that the highest interest of the first Somme battlefield lies between the main National Roads served by motor-buses. The only truly satisfactory way of visiting these fields is by leaving the main roads and to see them on foot, making use of the ready facility of the bus services connected with Amiens north and south. The tour can be extended from Péronne by continuing beyond Villers Carbonnel to Roye. But I suggest that such a tour would be too long and would do little justice to the battlefield or be satisfactory to the traveller.

In fact, throughout it is recommended to the visitor that, if his time is limited, he should view one or two points only, rather than attempt a *grand tour* to cover the whole field. For example, as will be seen from the text, to proceed by bus to Courcelette and then to walk to High Wood and back through Mametz to Albert, or to take this in easy stages by private car, is to obtain a full and lasting impression of the whole battlefield ; while the total distance of walking would not exceed five or six miles. For those who have time to spare, and who are bent also on leisure, there are excellent inns both at Albert and Péronne ; and there is much to see and to do.

This area, triangulating upon the towns of Amiens, Albert and Roye, covers the battlefield of 1916.

A battlefield of especial interest to those associated with the old British Regular Army, the Americans, and of course France itself, lies between the River Aisne and the Marne, triangulating upon the cities of Soissons, Rheims and Château Thierry. From Amiens the traveller may go south through Noyon to Soissons, which should serve as his base. The points of highest interest for the British visitor follow the course of the River Aisne. Château Thierry is some twenty miles south of Soissons, and is a centre for an American pilgrimage, as are also St. Mihiel farther south and Epéhy to the north.

The base for a third tour, to view especially the battlefields of 1914 and 1918, should be Péronne; and the area to be covered is described by the towns of Epéhy, St. Quentin and Ham. The fiercest fighting in this region took place around Epéhy, a stronghold of the Hindenburg Line which traversed this village, proceeding south to St. Quentin. From Epéhy the traveller goes south through Hargicourt and Bellenglise to St. Quentin. He may return to Péronne through Vermand, passing through villages which witnessed the heroic defence by British troops in March, 1918. Or he may continue south-west to Ham, across other battlefields. Ham itself was of great strategic importance during the retreat from Mons. The traveller may also choose either the northern or the southern section of the whole battle area, utilizing the Vermand–St. Quentin route as the dividing line. The distance which he would cover by taking one route or the other would be some fifty miles; and he should allow about five hours for the journey.

The Battles of the Somme are linked also with the important city of Bapaume, which was the head-quarters of Prince Rupprecht of Bavaria. Bapaume is only eleven miles from Albert; and, with good hotels, it provides a base from which to visit the battlefield of Arras, 1917, and of Cambrai in November of that year. But of the two, Arras may be found to be a more convenient centre, focusing as it does three battlefields—that of Bapaume, that of Cambrai and the Battle of Arras itself. From Arras, one route is to take the Douai road, across the bridge over the River Scarpe, at one time in No-Man's-Land, and thence to Gavrelle and Oppy, scenes of tremendous fighting in April, 1917, and of the British defence in March, 1918. Beyond this point the traveller enters the area of the British advance in September, 1918, towards Douai. From this interesting city, the southerly road to Cambrai would be taken, and it follows the line of the German defence captured in October, 1918. The return to Arras would be through Marquion, a distance of twenty-two miles; and the cemeteries running north and south of this village well mark the original front line. The total distance of this journey would be some sixty miles.

Another route, also served by the motor-bus, is to go outwards through Monchy to Vis-en-Artois. The river Sensée traverses this village, and to the south ran the Hindenburg Line of March, 1917, so fiercely stormed by British troops. The whole area to the south, through Croisilles and Boiry, is filled with rich memories and there are many cemeteries. The main road leads on to Cambrai; and the return can be made through Bapaume, from whence, if not previously seen, it is but a short tour through Les Bœufs, of bitter memory, to High Wood and thence through Bapaume on to the main Arras road.

Gommecourt, and the terrain fought over by the left wing of the First Battle of the Somme are passed, and to the right lie the villages of St. Léger and Hénin, which played an important part in the Battle of Arras.

From Cambrai the journey can be extended farther through Marquion and Gouzeaucourt to Fins, and then back from Equancourt to Bapaume. As with the area previously described, the centres of highest interest lie in between the main National Roads. The visitor who wishes to obtain the best impression of these battlefields is well advised to go to Fontaine les Croisilles, where old entrenchments yet remain, as they do at Gommecourt also, and to observe the panorama from this point; or to visit Bourlon, a centre for the "Battle of the Tanks"; or to make only the short journey to Fampoux.

Arras is also the most comfortable centre from which to visit Vimy Ridge; while being only twelve miles distant from the town of Lens, the battlefields of Loos are also conveniently to be visited from this base.

The ancient city of Béthune should certainly be seen, for it is peculiarly reminiscent of the early ventures of Kitchener's Army upon which was framed Britain's military might. Béthune is also the centre from which the villages and cemeteries represented by the Battle of the Lys, April, 1918, can be visited; and Armentières itself, connected by public services, is less than twenty miles distant. The battlefield of Neuve Chapelle lies only seven miles to the east; and those of Festubert, Ginchy and La Bassée are all within ten miles radius. Loos, where fought the "First Hundred Thousand," is only twelve miles to the south-east. Undoubtedly the best tour from Béthune is to Estaires, and from thence to follow the road to Lens, on either side of which ran the front lines of 1914 to 1918, smothered with cemeteries and memorials. The return to Béthune would be across the battlefield of Loos, through Vermelles, a total distance of less than fifty miles, and accomplished comfortably within five hours.

Cambrai will serve as a base for those desiring to revisit the battlefield of Le Cateau, 1914, and of the tremendous fighting between Valenciennes and Le Cateau in the late autumn of 1918. The distance between Cambrai and Le Cateau is some fifteen miles, and from thence there are a number of roads going north along which points of interest may be visited.

If the traveller has time, or may be more immediately interested in Armentières, a town peculiarly associated with the Old Army, he will find that it serves as a good centre from which to visit Loos, but especially the famous battle-grounds of 1914 and of early 1915 and of the stout defence in April, 1918, in the Battle of the Lys. Within three or four miles of Armentières lies the old trench line, the first dug in 1914. From Fromelles in the south, to Messines in the north, the line is well marked by many cemeteries; while such villages as Neuve Église and Meteren near by recall the heroism of the British Army with its "back to the wall," repelling the German onslaught in 1918. Almost any cemetery in the neighbourhood can be visited on foot from Armentières; and if the traveller elects to make this visit, he will experience on the *pavé* roads the marching and counter-marching of both the first and the last British Army which saved the Allies from defeat. Moreover, as history recalls, Armentières is a friendly city and will repay a visit. A short motor-tour, filled with interest, would travel north through Ploegsteert to Messines, and thence south-east, passing many cemeteries with curious English names, to Houplines. The road from this point runs south to Bois Grenier and then to Fleurbaix and Fromelles, from whence the traveller would strike the Béthune road back to Armentières. The total distance of this tour would be some thirty miles.

Ypres is the centre of interest which none can resist. Indeed it has become almost the Mecca for the pilgrim; and in its immediate neighbourhood are great numbers of points of interest, of cemeteries and memorials. The warrior returning to the scene of his battles will know whither to travel. It may be north to Langemarck or east to Passchendaele, to Polygon Wood and Zonnebeke, to Zillebeke and Larch Wood; or south to Voormezeele and Wytschaete. He may wish to see Mont Kemmel and Mont des Cats, or to go farther afield as far as Bailleul; or perhaps to visit Poperinghe, to the west, or to see Nieuport on the coast. Such a traveller must prepare his own Itinerary. No one visiting Ypres can see everything, though since all points of interest are encompassed within a short distance of a radius of eight miles, it is not difficult to see much, and to obtain a general impression and view of these battlefields.

I suggest the visitor should proceed eastwards through the Menin Gate to Potijze, and follow the road which leads to Tyne Cotts cemetery and thence to Passchendaele. From the high point of the ridge which runs due south, a superb panorama is obtained, covering the greater part of the bitter fighting which took place around Ypres between 1914 and the Armistice in 1918. The distance to Passchendaele is just over seven miles from Ypres. Again, the traveller may proceed south, through Dickebusch, La Clytte, Locre to Bailleul. This latter city, almost wholly destroyed in 1918, is the very fulcrum of the Battle of the Lys, and will serve as a centre from which to visit Meteren, Neuve Église and Armentières. Another road going east leads to Menin. The Battle of the Menin Road, September 1917, was an epic struggle.

The traveller on foot might well pass through Hooge as far as the Memorial of the 19th Infantry Brigade, which marks such famous battle scenes as Inverness Copse and Stirling Castle. He should then strike north across country to Polygon Wood; and he will pass over ground which in the War years was pockmarked with shell-holes beyond belief. He follows the ridge named "Tower Hamlets," captured by Londoners on the 26th September, 1917, and then joins the Passchendaele Road about one mile from Tyne Cotts cemetery, and then returns to Ypres. The distance is twelve miles, but the tour well repays the trouble; and of course it can be achieved also by motor-car. Another tour from Ypres selects the Warneton Road, passes beside Wytschaete; and from Warneton turns between Ploegsteert or Messines, and then continues through Neuve Église to Kemmel and thence back to Ypres. The distance would be about thirty miles; and the area is one of extraordinary interest, recalling famous actions during all the four years of the Great War.

For those who have no direct association with the battlefields, but who desire to obtain an abiding impression of the country over which the battles of the Great War surged, I suggest a visit to Ypres and from thence the tour to Passchendaele. An impression perhaps fuller is that of the Somme battlefield to be obtained by journeying to Amiens and from thence to Albert and Bapaume, towns convenient as halting-places; and from either one of these to go to High Wood. Arras may be chosen for a third centre, with a visit to Croisilles and up the valley of the Sensée River from this village. The visitor with leisure can well make a holiday centre at Picquigny on the River Somme, or at Corbie, also on the river, amid superb scenery. Or, if he is prepared to leave behind city civilization, he will find excellent hospitality in almost any one of the small towns and villages of Picardy and amid the attractive surroundings of Cassel in Flanders.

These brief notes suggesting an itinerary should be read in conjunction with and amplified by reference to the text itself. The Index at the end provides a reference to towns and villages. In planning a tour of the battlefields, it is suggested that the reader should refer to the text and to the maps; and it will be found that the keepers of the cemeteries are well informed, and are invariably courteous and helpful.

The peasant population, as a rule, has very little knowledge concerning the events which took place on the battlefields. A note of warning may here be given concerning vendors of " souvenirs." Such salesmen are not drawn from the peasant population, and some of their practices can only be described as ghoulish. They have appeared unfortunately at the main points of interest, and should be passed by.

The notes with this Itinerary have been introduced to indicate the spirit in which the traveller should visit the battlefields ; and it is further suggested that sections of this book may be read prior to each tour ; or that, by reference to the Index, passages may be read during halts as the tour proceeds.

CHAPTER I

KHAKI AND SKY-BLUE

The Picard in history—Peasant life—Character—French contribution
—Immense sacrifices—Allied cohesion—British adaptability—Griefs
and grievances—The charm of Picardy—Picard courtesy and hospitality.

HUNDREDS of books relating the experience of
British, German, and American troops in Picardy
have been published. Yet in scarcely one is there
even a passing reference to the character of the
people among whom the soldiers, sometimes when
actually participating in battle, but always in reserve
and rest, spent their moments of ease and recreation.

Some poets among soldiers have been arrested
for a moment by the beauty of Picardy. But, even
for these, the sheer horror of its despoliation by the
monstrous cruelty of war has pictured this fair
countryside as only a wraith hovering over the
carnage of the battlefield. The peasant life, almost
extinguished by billet and by picket, by concentrations, by evacuations, has escaped notice.

Yet the character of the Picard strangely infected
British soldiers during the Great War, and it has
endured to refurnish the devastated regions with
their natural beauties. And this last is cause for
astonishment when it is remembered that a large
part of Picardy was subjected to a plan of systematic
destruction by Germany. The *Berliner Tageblatt*
wrote of the Somme region as " a desert incapable
for a long time of producing the things necessary
to life." Yet it is difficult to find any visible traces
of the appalling upheaval which crumbled towns
and villages to dust, laid low the woods, and pock-

marked nearly every square yard of an immense area. For, such is the patience and the aggressive zeal for labour of those of this countryside, that where men of less courage and endurance would have feared the task of reincarnating those pitted and scarred wastes as the source of a prosperous agriculture, the peasant has succeeded.

In his origins the Picard shares much in common with the English, themselves a people of heterogeneous racial origin, though long since identified by racial type. The people of Picardy have their ancestry in the Belgæ, a mixed race, who, crossing the English Channel, also spread throughout Wessex and Sussex and the Weald of Kent. Julius Cæsar found the Belgæ to be most intractable, obstinate and ever covertly, and openly, in rebellion against Roman rule. Cæsar considered the Belgæ to be Celts, but more probably, as is supported by other authorities, they were of mixed Celtic and Teutonic origin, a suggestion which would explain the sympathy, immediate and natural, which sprang up between British soldiers and their Picard hosts, that even linguistic difficulties did not obstruct. Nor, once the shock of invasion and the hate of disturbance of liberty had been overcome, was the Picard unfriendly towards the German. Something of Teuton in him leaped from past tradition, making the bond of an oppressive, military control ripen into one of unaffected friendship, to which the habit of fatalism, common to all peasants, added its mellowing touch.

The peasantry, as indeed was necessary, were always subordinate to military control, against which their character, as in the Roman epoch, and enduring throughout twenty centuries, was always in revolt. Yet, their hardihood, patience, endurance and frugality exercised a marked influence upon the campaign. No one ever saw the Picard in panic. True to his characteristic, he was obstinate in asserting his rights and liberties even when such notions of equity and of liberty conflicted with peril to his own person and possessions.

The Picard continued to plough under shell-fire, to tend his crops even where bullets sometimes lashed the waving corn, to cling to his tenement even when its roof had been torn and walls gashed by gun-fire. His house and barns were filled with soldiery, his fields picketed with horses, his pastures turned into parade- and play-grounds. Yet, year after year, his family herded into some corner of the farm-house, his cattle mixed with mules, his granaries bulging with soldiers and their equipment, with dogged persistence the Picard carried on his farming operations as if the war did not exist.

" *C'est la guerre!* " he would stoically exclaim with a shrug of the shoulders, and continue then to act as if no war had ever come to obstruct the delivery of grain in its season, the upturning of the root-crop, or the breeding of animals. Certain traits in the character of the Picard are distinctive. He is scrupulously honest, and herein he expresses himself as do all true peasants. Indeed, as everywhere, what is sometimes called up-to-date commerce and smart business has succeeded in degrading the beauty of peasant life—truth, strict honesty, the family, and religion. But for two thousand years Picardy, although swept by tramping armies, has successfully resisted every invasion; and that which would sap its traditional culture is well safeguarded by the Church.

The Picard is also politeness personified. He will resist brusqueness of manner. " Indeed, the only way to win them consists in making them appreciate that one esteems their courage, their tenacity, and their courtesy (for they pride themselves much on this). Demonstrate kindness and confidence in the people and they will contribute all in their power, and with a good grace. But they will not suffer either personal injury or violence." So wrote Pierra de Marca in 1635 to the Comte d'Estrades of another independent peasantry, his Catalan charge. Nor is this ancient appreciation inappropriate as a summary of this other peasant race of France, the Picards. To hector and to browbeat them, to ride roughshod over their rights was to invite a sullen obstinacy and resistance. To respect these rights, to render courtesies, to demonstrate kindness and courtesy, was to win their hearts and the contribution of all in their power with overwhelming generosity. And so British Generals and soldiers would fight their battles in the morning and help the farmers of Picardy to stack their corn at eventide, and the peasants gave up their beds, their restricted, often even meagre, produce, to satisfy a weary body, to gladden the heart of an ally.

You might see a group of officers seated in an inn, for example, in the Café Alexandre or the Hôtel de la Poste at Corbie, filling its every corner, occupying every chair and table, their slightest wish and whim gratified by kindly hostesses. And in the hamlets and farmsteads, around the kitchen fire, would always be discovered an ever-changing, yet how changeless, group of soldiers, partaking of the family hospitality, enjoying very fully " a home from home."

The Picard is short-tempered, and the wonder is that throughout the War he suffered so much with such amazing tolerance. The patois which he speaks, with all its amazing varieties almost from one town to another, is Celtic in origin, and this may account for his special warmth of feeling towards the Scot. The patois of Montreuil, Sir Douglas Haig's headquarters, differs from that of the Somme battlefield between Beaumont Hamel and Péronne in as great a degree as did the notions upon tactical possibility differ between those at G.H.Q. and the men in the front line ! The patois possesses curious mixtures and accentuations of Roman, Teutonic and English expressions due no doubt to the various invasions of these fiercely contested fields.

But be it noted that though Picardy has always been the battle-ground, the peasants have never been the aggressors. Always have they resisted invasion, and throughout their character has remained unchanged. They remain a proud, independent, kindly, courteous, hard-working, godly people, whose fund of anecdote, to those who understand their tongue, is as pawky as is the proverbial wit of the Celtic Scot.

The Picard conforms to no definite racial type,

C

though on the whole he is fair compared with the southern French. No people have clung more faithfully to their Church, and whether it be in the vast cathedrals at Amiens, Beauvais and Abbeville or in the most remote village church, upon Sundays, from dawn until the hour of High Mass, there can always be seen a procession threading its way to Divine worship.

On 27th August, 1914, the advanced guards of the British and German armies encountered a host of people attired in clean linen, or in sombre black, forming such processions on their way from their devotions; and each Sunday, though a godless soldiery, disporting itself in the fields of the " Rest Areas," rent the air with the cry of its games, the village curé in quiet tones ministered to his patient, faithful flock.

England and Scotland have been variously associated closely with the history of Picardy. The battles of Crécy and of Azincourt and Marlborough's campaigns are landmarks in this story. But less familiar are other details in the tale of a growth side by side. During the interminable wars of the Middle Ages, Amiens was always warm in its sympathy for the France of French kings. Not so the outlying districts, whose peasantry, with much prudence, in disputes none of their choosing or interest, preferred the winning side.

The Picard is strongly republican in sentiment, preferring the increasingly doubtful benefits of what passes for democracy to the impositions of earlier Seigneurs, whose strictures have passed into current legend, with memories of the hated *corvée*. But there is no doubt about the patriotic fervour of the Picard, expressed in devotion to his soil and to his Church. He is possessed of a very real sense of obligation to the soil from which he springs and which supports him. That is his patriotism. Nor will he tolerate interference with his rights. Any kind of imposed constitution which threatens his prized liberty, by whatever name it may be heralded, is sure to meet with an instinctive and stout resistance.

Of mediæval history, it was at Abbeville in 1259 that Henry III of England ceded the province of Normandy to France; and in 1527 that Francis I and Cardinal Wolsey concluded a military alliance against the Emperor Charles V. In the glorious cathedral of St. Vulfran, whose front is almost identical with that of Westminster Abbey, the marriage took place between Mary Tudor, daughter of Henry VII, and Louis XII in 1514. At Abbeville, also, upon the belfry—and the belfry in Picardy as in Flanders is the symbol of independence—is a bas-relief in honour of the patriot of Abbeville, Ringois, who, taken prisoner in the revolt of 1368 and thrown into the prison of Dover Castle, was pressed to accept Edward III as his liege lord. Typical of the Picard, Ringois refused to do so, and leaped, or perhaps was thrown, from the window of his prison, in order that at least his spirit should suffer no imprisonment.

A short distance from Abbeville, along the bank of the Somme towards Amiens, lies the village of Pont Rémy, so often billeted by British troops in rest from battle. It was here that Edward III attempted the passage of the Somme. A fifteenth-century château, situated on an island, yet remains, whose glory is that its defenders defeated three thousand English men-at-arms and forced them to retreat.

Perhaps it may appear as something of a paradox to suggest that the histories of the Great War sometimes seem to forget that it was fought in France. From Armentières, north of the River Lys, on the Belgian frontier, as far south as the Alps, where the soil of France and of Switzerland meet in the mountains, the battle-front was French, and all the battle-fields are coloured with the heroic defence of France against the invader. No matter what were the political causes of the Great War, or upon whom must rest its responsibility, the main burden of defence, at least during the first two years of the War, fell upon the French.

The slaughter-house of the Somme, with its many memorials; the fields of Picardy and Flanders, so grim with British cemeteries; Soissons and Rheims, immortal as the scenes of British feats of arms; Château Thierry, eloquent in its testimony to the American contribution, these may overshadow the sacrifice of France in the long years of her peril. Nor must one overlook the fact that for France, Germany was the hereditary enemy. No matter how France might be divided against itself in feudal contests between the dukes and nobles of history, the French had always rallied when the princes and barons of Germany assailed the gates of France. And in later years, when Frenchmen fought against the English invaders under Marlborough, they fought also against Germans who took common cause with the invader. But France was also an aggressor, and it would be a poor compliment to the advance of civilization to suggest that no nation in its turn had suffered defeat because it challenged the stability upon which inevitably civilization must rest. In the Napoleonic wars, France became the aggressor. But here again, at Austerlitz and Jena or at Waterloo, on whichever side might be found the islanders of Britain, the arms of France were pitted against those of Germany.

Men may be inclined to think of the Somme, of Arras, of La Bassée, of Loos and of Armentières as battlefields exclusively British in which the French played no part, and to confine French operations to such scenes as those of Verdun, the Marne, and Hartmannsweilerkopf. But there was not one yard of the British front, not one battlefield, upon which the sons of France did not shed their blood.

The Departments of the Pas de Calais, Somme, Aisne, Marne and Vosges, throughout the four years of war, witnessed the passage and repassage of the Armies of France. After 1914, the British Army held the front of the Pas de Calais, and after 1915, that, also, of the Somme. During the early days of 1914, British Brigades had fought in those of the Aisne and Marne; and everywhere in these Departments, the Memorials and Cemeteries to the British may contribute a first impression that the efforts of the British empire upon foreign soil were greater than those who claimed it as their land.

But while in the Battle of the Frontiers, between October and November, 1914, the British suffered a loss of 84,785 men, the French casualties reached the enormous total of 854,000. During the period of stabilization between December, 1914 and January, 1915, the British losses were 17,621 men and those of France 254,000. Thousands among the losses of France were killed as the armies fell back step by step before the invader; and their burial-place will never be known. An examination of the statistics of the losses on the Western Front reveals the fact that except during the period July to October, 1916, at the Battle of the Somme; between April and July, 1917, wherein were fought the Battles of the Chemin des Dames, of Arras and of Messines, and between August and December, 1917, which included the British offensives at Passchendaele and Cambrai, the losses of the French always exceeded those of the British.

The French casualties in killed, missing, prisoners, and wounded reached a total of 4,938,000 [1] men; while the British losses on the Western Front were 2,706,000. The sacrifices of France, therefore, on the Western Front were nearly double those of Great Britain. The losses in the first months of 1914 were nearly twice as great as those in the succeeding period. In the First Battle of Champagne, in February, March, 1915, the French casualties amounted to 240,000: in the Second Battle of Artois, April to June, 1915, to 449,000. In the Second Battle of Champagne, in September, November, 1915, 410,000; and in defence against the German offensive between March and June, 1918, 483,000; while between July and November,

[1] Official Return of the Chamber, Resolution of Deputy Moran, March, 1922.

1918, to secure the freedom of their land from the invader, France sacrificed a further 531,000 men.

The extraordinary generosity of the British and Empire peoples in setting up memorials and in laying out cemeteries upon foreign soil certainly does suggest to the casual observer that the British sacrifices far exceeded those of France. These figures belie any such impression. Even among great numbers of British soldiers who took part in the War, knowledge as to the French contribution to the Allied cause on the Western Front is almost wholly absent. For reasons of supply, control and direction, and indeed also of language, the British Armies, as they grew in numbers, were segregated, both in line and in depth, from their allies; and except on the extreme flanks, had little knowledge of their life and operations. It was only during moments of terrible drama and of the utmost peril that British and French troops came to have any real knowledge of one another and to appreciate the qualities inherent in the two races.

In August and September, 1914, the British and French Armies became inextricably mixed together in the Battles of the Aisne and of the Marne. One witnessed columns and columns of men in blue uniform surging over the battlefield; and as the New Armies from Great Britain began to take over the line in 1915, the grim remains of French heroism met them at every point. In those early days, as in the later vast struggles on the Somme or at Ypres, there was no time to bury the dead. The single trench at La Bassée was piled with French corpses. Skeletons and the remains of clothing and equipment were dug deep into the crumbling parapets. The familiar " Old Boots Trench " in front of La Bassée was so named from the booted legs which thrust themselves from a front-line parapet, and which, always under heavy fire, could not be removed.

Again, in Artois, while the lines before Armentières and Festubert were being stabilized, British Infantry were supported by French Artillery, the matchless ·75 Batteries. On the Somme in July, 1916, the ponderous French transport appeared on all the roads, immense camions, and all kinds of curious carts drawn by shaggy little horses, harnessed, as it seemed, in most haphazard fashion. But while at almost every point the British attack was held on the 1st July, that of the French, astride the River Somme itself, leaped forward, recapturing a huge tract of French soil with thousands of prisoners and guns.

A great military authority has written : " Indestructible cohesion, best of all qualities which an armed body can possess, is based not alone upon the hereditary resolution, but on mutual confidence and respect." [1] For political reasons, and not least due to the temperamental differences between the British and French Army Commanders, no such cohesion existed in the earlier stages of the War. Indeed Marlborough, fighting over these same battlefields, commanding a strange medley of Englishmen, Dutchmen, Hanoverians, Danes, Wurtembergers and Austrians, secured a greater cohesion throughout his Army than did the Allies until the moment of extreme peril produced the man, Foch.

While politicians still struggled for a formula with

[1] *The Science of War*, by Col. G. F. R. Henderson.

which to invest the authority of the Generalissimo, the French troops, shoulder to shoulder with the British, fought over their earlier battlefields in Northern France and for the defence of the remnants of Belgium. To stem the tide which overwhelmed the Fifth Army on the Somme, French guns came in support. While the British line cracked on the Lys, French armoured cars, as the vanguard of Divisions, came to the support of the wearied, weakened British Divisions. On the 27th April, 1918, at Mont Kemmel, the 28th French Infantry, fighting beside the British, perished almost to a man ; and this is but an example of the contribution of France to the British Army in its hour of peril.

By contrast, of equal contribution was that of the already shattered British Corps beside Soissons in June, 1918, fighting upon the old British battlefields of the Aisne and the Marne, when the example of young Territorial Divisions upheld the French Army when it was well-nigh overwhelmed by Germany in her final bid for victory.

It was at this moment that cohesion, quite indestructible, between the Armies of France and Britain revealed itself.

It was only after nearly four years of war that the British and French Armies truly realized themselves as comrades-in-arms serving a great cause. Understanding had its origin in mutual sacrifices, mutually shared. How true it is that the darkest hour precedes the dawn. The bloody slopes of Kemmel, even more the death agonies of the Chemin des Dames and of the Aisne, produced that mutual confidence and respect which Marshal Foch could then temper into the steel of final victory. It is indeed a curious reflection that the so nearly won victory for German arms in 1918 produced the essential cohesion in the ranks of the Allies. In the great forward sweep which followed so swiftly after retreat and almost defeat, the recriminations and distrust which so often had characterized the relations between the British and French Armies in the earlier stages of the War completely disappeared. With rare generosity Marshal Foch paid his tribute to Sir Douglas Haig, whose striking series of victories between July, 1918, and the Armistice astonished even the most optimistic among the critics.

There has been a growing tendency among a certain section of politicians, whose views attain the maximum of publicity, to suggest that some kind of international order will supersede the nations as the world knows and recognizes them to-day.

If the battlefields of France have any lesson for the historian they are an eloquent denial of the truth of any such assertion. The British soldier served for four years in France. Adaptable as he is, for the time being he assumed something of the customs and of the graces of the land of his exile. But so soon as he returned to his native land he shook off such little of the influence of France which had made its superficial impression and again became the Englishman, the Scot, the man of Wales or of Ireland. During four years Picardy and Flanders contained a population which in many towns and villages greatly outnumbered the native inhabitants. Such centres as Poperinghe,

Amiens, St. Pol became almost English cities and the authority in many villages was entirely British. Yet despite this invasion nothing remains of British influence, excepting kindly remembrance, and scarcely one English word has been added to the vocabulary of the inhabitants. Nevertheless, so long as the War lasted the influence of the French people upon the British soldiers was considerable.

War, of necessity, imposes restrictions upon liberty. No matter how friendly may be an invading army as allies, the restrictions and impositions of military exigencies must provoke annoyance and irritation among the civilian population who remain. Grievances are accentuated through linguistic difficulties which produce all kinds of misunderstandings. In France, the *Maire* of a Commune would find himself stripped of authority by aliens, whether British or Germans, who had no time to wait upon ceremony.

Farmers and housewives throughout four years found themselves compelled to submit to requisitions and billetings, disorganizing their accustomed life. But to understand how especially annoying to the French of Picardy was the intrusion of the invading Armies is to understand something of the character of the people of these districts. The peasant's idea of happiness has always been to fight his way to the purchase of a little farm, and in Picardy even the poorest is possessed of his own plot of land.

A recent Official Return of cultivated land in France reports 5,550,000 distinct properties, and 5,000,000 of these are under six acres in size.

In Picardy, the peasants for the most part are

cleanly and well-to-do; and British soldiers in their
billeting will remember the beds as being almost
universally immaculate, and the food served in
farms and inns as being excellent. The villages
and farms still sustain such a tradition, and the
traveller is always allotted a room as if he were the
honoured guest; while the landlord, often well-
to-do and well-educated, will wait cheerily at table
while his wife cooks; and the host and hostess treat
their guests like old friends.

Men who have revisited their war-time billets
have discovered that they have been held in a
kindly remembrance; and travellers are only their
own enemies who do not open their hearts to the
frankness and charm of character in the French to
which the whole system of their education tends.
There are villages which for years were held in
German occupation, wherein also the German
visitors, despite the cruelty of invasion, are yet held
in affectionate regard, and this is especially true of
those who embraced the Catholic faith. The customs and observances of Eastern France never failed
to impress especially the educated among the British
Armies.

The extraordinary good manners among the
lower orders may certainly be traced to the extreme
politeness with which they are treated by their
superiors, perhaps in marked contrast to English
custom, especially since the industrial era. No
Frenchman would think of being aggrieved by
having to sit down at the *table d'hôte* with his chauf-
feur, or would think of addressing him without
the prefix of a " *Monsieur*." Servants are always

treated as part of the family, and pains are taken by their masters to adapt themselves to any characteristics which it may not be possible to change. Hence the proverb " *le maître fait le valet*." In the same way the servant accepts his master's interest as his own, and he gladly undertakes any office or fulfils any duties beyond those for which he is engaged, if there is the slightest reason for it. The peasants of France have, therefore, in its highest form, preserved the aristocratic ideal. One observes precisely similar characteristics and customs in remote British country districts, in Bavaria, and in Indian village life. Indeed, the aristocratic ideal, perfected democracy, exists among all nations wherein there is a vigorous peasant and yeoman life.

The peasants of Picardy may be poor, but they may also be the equals of the greatest *Seigneur*. England has almost lost its yeoman and peasant class, but in France it is the background of the national life. Many more aids to making the lives of the humbler classes pleasant are to be found in France than in England. Every provincial town possesses its shady walks and promenades, where bands play gratuitously, and even large villages have their enclosures of lilac, plane and fir trees, where open-air benches equate the seats of English public-houses. It was in these pleasant shady enclosures, as in Corbie, that British soldiers were accustomed to assume something of the French mode of life. British bands supplied the music, while the French elders and the children left behind would come every evening after their work to watch and join in the gossip.

Despite the annoyances to the French peasantry they would open their hearts to all and any, except those who showed a contempt for their customs and displayed a brusqueness of manner towards their modest requirements. A charge often made against the French peasantry was that they are exceedingly avaricious, but such was beside the truth. Careful, prodigal of necessity in their expenditure, with an eye to every detail in the establishment of the small holding, its house, its fences and its modest pasture, naturally enough the peasant would not tolerate the destruction or spoliation of some apparent detail of importance to his eyes. To the Englishman, with his motto " Time is money," the often petty objections of small farmers to requisitions appeared exaggerated and absurd. But in France they say " Time is pleasure " ; and herein lies a great philosophic and economic truth, for time is not money, though it is nearly everything else.

Behold, then, these French villages centred around Armentières, Béthune, St. Pol, Arras and Amiens, in which throughout the War years a British population, perhaps more than two million men, lived and moved and had their being. Fresh and adventurous, they came from the English training camps, surging through the villages, filling the streets, the small houses, halls and barns, ignorant of the customs of the country, seeing unfamiliar sights, relaxed from the home conventions and un-tutored in those of any other land, regarding the affairs of the French peasants as some kind of an exhibition at which to wonder or of which to make fun, as the mood took them. The young spring grass, carefully manured, became a football ground, and if farmers invoked the heavens for relief, they prayed also for their unwelcome guests.

Everything about peasant life from dawn until dusk and long after was an aggravation. The English mules gnawed the bark from trees and destroyed them, poultry went missing, root-crops were unearthed and corn was trampled down. Peasants were knocked up at all hours of night and there was no one to whom they could appeal for the mitigation of intolerance. Week followed week and month followed month without response to the desperate needs of the inhabitants. And yet no appeal was made in vain to their kindness or for the granting of some favour. Picture to yourself, then, a population which from day to day and from week to week did not know what fresh humiliation would fall upon them, to what new inconvenience they would be subjected, who often did not know whether bombs by night would blow them from their beds or a stream of shells would churn up their pastures and lay their cattle low; who were obliged to meet every day men who knew little of their tongue and nothing of their customs, whose first and only thought could be of their own comfort and rest and recreation and for whom the requirements of a farmer were only intolerable. As the British troops swept by in retreat in August, 1914, only those who received the promises of these peasants to guard the graves of their fallen brothers can realize with what faithfulness they carried out their pledges, as is revealed from the fact that many of these graves were tended throughout the War until victory restored them to France.

The traveller or pilgrim who wanders over the battlefields and sees the neat villages which have arisen on the ruins of those destroyed can little realize the amazing patience and unfailing courtesy of a peasantry eternally harried, moved hither and thither with the swaying of the battle, hurried in retreat with their scant belongings, their houses turned inside out by numberless strangers, making themselves adaptable to their own compatriots, to Englishmen, to Americans and Australians, to Indians, Senegalese, and to Chinese coolies. Among most men one would ordinarily suppose that such endurance would have left a mark, and that the imposition of these years had obliterated for all time any sense of hospitality towards the traveller. But those who revisit the battlefields do find the population as eager with kindly hospitality as they were when without complaint they surrendered the comforts of their homes to those who fought the battles. Whatever were the political causes of the War, it will be an ill thing indeed if Germans who received no mean hospitality and kindness at the hands of the peasantry of France forget these courtesies in the humiliations of the peace. But we have learned what were the true causes; and Franco-German friendship will grow every day.

With such a reflection one remembers the *Curés*,

GASSED

The Dressing-Station at Le Bac-du-Sud, on the Doullens–Arras Road, August, 1918. Gassed cases arrived in parties of about six men, led by an orderly.

John S. Sargent, R.A.

A RATION PARTY OF THE 4TH BLACK WATCH AT THE BATTLE OF NEUVE CHAPELLE, 1915

Joseph Gray.

who, albeit French, were priests of that Supernational, not International, Church which knows no frontiers and which everywhere embraces Christian men. The ministry of the *Curés* among their own flocks was continued, but it extended itself often also among the invaders, whether Allies or enemies. The *Curé*, however erudite, as indeed he often is, lives simply among the peasantry, sharing the trials of their day-to-day life ; and though anticlericalism has swept over Picardy, fostered by the Press, few Picards do not send their children to their first Communion as the great event of life when the child passes to the stage of youth.

As are most peasant people, the Picards are a moral race. A famous Scottish minister, peeved by the waywardness of his Border peasant folk, adjured them " to leap from Delilah's lap into the arms of Abraham," and such a metaphor may sometimes be wise counsel in any village of Picardy. But the sanctity of family life makes a very strong claim upon the Picard, and such pointed admonition would here seldom be called for : and of other vices they have few.

The simplicity of the *Curé* suggests, also, by way of parable, the process by which stage by stage exaltation is reached, as we see it in the glory of Amiens Cathedral, the very soul of Picardy. Here, man has offered as a shrine, at the footstool of the Divine Throne, all the splendours of art and the superlative qualities of architecture, set amid the sparse downs and valleys where man must toil mightily to produce the necessities of life.

D

In reflection, finally, it is not without some abiding sense of honour that we British may reflect that many of the new villages of the war-devastated areas owe their rebuilding to the generosity of English burghers.

CHAPTER II

THE SOMME—A FIRST SURVEY

The first battle—Unparalleled preparations—The bombardment, 1st July,
1916—German eye-witness account of the attack—Gains and losses
—Amiens Cathedral—Galignani's observations, 1827—Historical notes.

THE First Battle of the Somme, 1916, presents one
of the greatest tragedies in all human history. As
the years have receded, as death has removed the
principal actors in the great drama, whose reputations,
for reasons of public policy, had to be protected, and
as the flood of literature, both official and unofficial,
dealing with the main events and with their detailed
story has become available, it is clear that the
battlefields of the Somme must for ever remain
those of shattered hopes and of unparalleled
disillusion.

The British Generals were certain of success,
despite the vague allusions as to the objectives by
Colonel Boraston, Lord Haig's official biographer.
The General Staff was supremely confident that the
German lines would be broken and that the invading
Armies would be rolled back for many miles. During the spring and early summer, farther south, the
French Armies had been engaged in fighting of the
utmost ferocity around Verdun, an epic which
testifies to the almost incredible gallantry of France
in defence of her own soil—" *Ils ne passeront pas !* "
—and to the equally brave assaults of numbers of
German Divisions. The sufferings of France inspired the new British Armies in their first great
test of war.

Those who took part in the Battle of the Somme

consisted for the most part of " Kitchener's Army," the flower of English manhood, who, in the new Divisions, and older reorganized Brigades, had appeared in the field since the shock of the ill-success at Loos, in the September of the preceding year. Sir Douglas Haig, possessed of a military reputation unknown to most, but familiar as a figure of martial bearing, trusted by his subordinates, had succeeded Sir John French, in whom confidence had been lost since the disasters at Neuve Chapelle and at Loos.

Preparations upon an hitherto unparalleled scale had been made for the battle. " To mystify and mislead " is one of the first principles of military strategy and tactics. The element of surprise is a law which no soldier, in theory, ignores. Yet under daily observations from balloons and by aircraft, new railways were laid down and roads constructed ; while immense dumps of munitions and war stores of all kinds were laid out beside the villages and in the fields in the battle zone. There were enormous concentrations of artillery. By night and day the cobbled National Roads thundered with motor and horse transport ; while vast armies of men, infantry— predominantly infantry—cavalry and the ancillary services poured into the villages and new encampments in the area between the River Ancre and the River Somme ; east of Amiens, Doullens and St. Pol, and west of the main German line which traced its well-nigh impregnable strength along the high ground which runs from Mont St. Quentin by Péronne, through Longueval, Martinpuich, Courcelette, Thiepval and Gommecourt Park, with its forward defences of entrenchments and communications, stretching towards the British lines three or four miles to the west.

Sir Douglas Haig in his Despatches wrote :

During nearly two years' preparation he (the enemy) had spared no pains to render these defences impregnable. The first and second systems each consisted of several lines of deep trenches, well provided with bomb-proof shelters and with numerous communication trenches connecting them. The front of the trenches in each system was protected by wire entanglements, many of them in two belts forty yards broad, built of iron stakes interlaced with barbed wire, often almost as thick as a man's finger.

The numerous woods and villages in and between these systems of defence had been turned into veritable fortresses. The deep cellars usually to be found in the villages, and the numerous pits and quarries common to a chalk country, were used to provide cover for machine guns and trench mortars. The existing cellars were supplemented by elaborate dug-outs, sometimes in two storeys, and these were connected up by passages as much as thirty feet below the surface of the ground. The salients in the enemy's line, from which he could bring enfilade fire across his front, were made into self-contained forts and often protected by mine-fields ; while strong redoubts and concrete machine-gun emplacements had been constructed in positions from which he could sweep his own trenches, should these be taken. The ground lent itself to good artillery observation on the enemy's part, and he had skilfully arranged for cross-fire by his guns.

These various systems of defence, with the fortified localities and other supporting points between them, were cunningly sited to afford each other mutual assistance and to admit of the utmost possible development of enfilade and flanking fire by machine guns and artillery. They formed, in short, not merely a series of successive lines, but one composite system of enormous depth and strength.

Behind his second system of trenches, in addition to woods, villages and other strong points prepared for defence, the enemy had several other lines already completed; and we had learnt from aeroplane reconnaissance that he was hard at work improving and strengthening these and digging fresh ones between them, and still farther back.

The reason for the choice of this ground for a test of strength was that it was believed that if the German lines could be broken at what appeared to be their strongest point, then the morale of the German Armies would be destroyed; and the victory of the Somme would be followed by a series of sharp and decisive victories. The optimism of the General Staff was unqualified, though Lord Rawlinson, commanding the Fourth Army, upon which fell the brunt of the attack, expressed his doubts as to success and as to the means adopted to attain it. Nor does Colonel Boraston make it clear in what period of time the High Command anticipated the " break through."

It is recorded that the Germans were unable to believe that the British seriously intended to develop their main attack against the Somme defences. Rather did they think that the elaborate preparations which they had observed were but a blind with which to force the German High Command to denude its front farther north of reserves and to concentrate them in the region of Douai and Bapaume, while the main British attack, with surprise, would seek to penetrate the German lines farther north. In result, when the British and French attack developed on the 1st July on a front of forty-five kilometres, the Germans, at the point of issue, had very few troops in immediate reserve; and yet, despite unexampled determination and gallantry, the British attack broke down everywhere, except on a front of eight miles, where it succeeded in establishing itself in the forward German lines and carrying the attack a mile or two beyond.

For a whole week prior to the 1st July, the German defences were subjected to an intense artillery bombardment. Hundreds of thousands of tons of shells were fired into the entrenchments. During this week the German histories record that it was almost impossible for any man to leave the depths of the deep dug-outs in order to seek sustenance for the wounded, for food or for water. A German eye-witness writing of these events says:

> The intense bombardment was realized by all to be a prelude to the infantry assault at last. The men in the dug-outs therefore waited ready, a belt full of hand grenades around them, gripping their rifles and listening for the bombardment to lift from the front defence zone on to the rear defences. It was of vital importance to lose not a second in taking up position in the open to meet the British infantry who would be advancing immediately behind the artillery barrage. Looking towards the British trenches through the long trench periscopes held up out of the dug-out entrances, there could be seen a mass of steel helmets above their parapet showing that their storm-troops were ready for the assault. At 7.30 a.m. the hurricane of shells ceased as suddenly as it had begun. Our men at once clambered up the steep shafts leading from the dug-outs to daylight and ran singly or in groups to the nearest shell craters. The machine guns were pulled out of the dug-outs and hurriedly placed into position, their crews dragging the heavy ammunition boxes up the steps and out to the guns. A rough firing

line was thus rapidly established. As soon as in position
a series of extended lines of British infantry were seen
moving forward from the British trenches. The first
line appeared to continue without end to right and left.
It was quickly followed by a second line, then a third and
fourth. They came on at a steady easy pace as if expect-
ing to find nothing alive in our front trenches. . . . The
front line, preceded by a thin line of skirmishers and
bombers, was now half-way across No-Man's-Land.

" Get ready ! " was passed along our front from crater
to crater, and heads appeared over the crater edges as
final positions were taken up for the best view and machine
guns mounted firmly in place. A few minutes later, when
the leading British line was within 100 yards, the rattle
of machine-gun and rifle fire broke out from along the
whole line of craters. Some fired kneeling so as to get
a better target over the broken ground, while others, in
the excitement of the moment, stood up regardless of
their own safety to fire into the crowd of men in front of
them. Red rockets sped up into the blue sky as a signal
to the artillery, and immediately afterwards a mass of
shells from the German batteries in rear tore through the
air and burst among the advancing lines. Whole sections
seemed to fall, and the rear formations, moving in closer
order, quickly scattered. The advance rapidly crumpled
under this hail of shells and bullets. All along the line
men could be seen throwing their arms into the air and
collapsing never to move again. Badly wounded rolled
about in their agony, and others less severely injured
crawled to the nearest shell-hole for shelter.

The British soldier, however, has no lack of courage,
and once his hand is set to the plough he is not easily
turned from his purpose. The extended lines, though
badly shaken and with many gaps, now came on all the
faster. Instead of a leisurely walk they covered the ground
in short rushes at the double. Within a few minutes the
leading troops had reached within a stone's throw of our
front trench, and while some of us continued to fire at
point-blank range, others threw hand grenades among
them. The British bombers answered back, while the
infantry rushed forward with fixed bayonets. The noise
of battle became indescribable. The shouting of orders
and the shrill British cheers as they charged forward

could be heard above the violent and intense fusillade of machine guns and rifles and the bursting bombs, and above the deep thunderings of the artillery and the shell explosions. With all this were mingled the moans and groans of the wounded, the cries for help and the last screams of death. Again and again the extended lines of British infantry broke against the German defence like waves against a cliff, only to be beaten back.

It was an amazing spectacle of unexampled gallantry, courage and bull-dog determination on both sides.[1]

This simple report is characteristic of what occurred along the whole British line. On the 1st July, of the fourteen British Divisions immediately engaged, 60,000 men had been lost, killed, wounded, or prisoners in the hands of the enemy; and the 1st July, 1916, remains as probably the greatest tragedy of all military history. There was never slaughter and loss on so great a scale.

It seems necessary as a prelude to a description of the Somme battlefields, and of what ensued in the following months, to present this picture of unparalleled preparation, of the immensity of the task presented to the attack and of disappointment indescribable. It is a remarkable testimony to the ardour and valour of British arms that despite the appalling reverse of the 1st July, the series of attacks which followed, with losses almost equally galling, were sustained with undiminished gallantry. And yet the optimism of the General Staff seems to have suffered no set-back from the first shattering blow to the Battle Plan. Colonel Boraston writes:

The events of July 1st . . . bore out the conclusions of the British Higher Command and amply justified the tactical methods employed.

---

[1] *Die Schwaben an der Ancre*, Gerster.

The machine gun had won the day, and one machine gun can mow down five hundred and even far more men within the space of a minute or two, as was again shown in April, 1918, when at Meteren, beside Bailleul, one British Machine Gun Battalion, holding a front of nearly three miles, decimated the assaults of eleven German Divisions.[1]

Although the Somme battlefield is pre-eminently concerned with the gigantic contest which commenced on the 1st July, 1916, and which petered out amid mud, morass and ruins, on the line which runs through Bouchavesnes, Le Transloy, High Wood and Gommecourt, in November, this area witnessed also fierce fighting in March, 1918, when the Germans overwhelmed the 5th Army, under General Gough, recapturing the whole and more of the ground wrested from them in 1916. The Germans were then only held at the very gates of Amiens by the heroic stand of the Australians at Villers Bretonneux. The losses to the British Army were not less than 50,000 men, including a number of Generals, while vast quantities of guns and stores fell into the hands of the enemy.

The Somme battlefields witnessed also the fiercest fighting of the great attack, under Marshal Foch as Generalissimo, in the victorious Allied thrust towards the east which culminated at Maubeuge, Mons and Le Cateau, the very point at which the British Armies had first engaged the enemy. Between the 8th August and the 11th November, 1918, the old battlefields of the Somme again thundered with gun-fire and were whipped by machine-gun fire. In

[1] *Warrior* (Chap. XIII), by Lt.-Col. G. S. Hutchison.

the first four days nearly 22,000 prisoners and four
hundred guns were captured east of Corbie and
Méricourt. Between the 21st and 31st August,
34,000 prisoners and 270 guns were captured in the
retaking of Albert and in the recapture of the whole of
the 1916 battlefields, carrying the line eastwards to
the redoubtable Hindenburg Line, lying ten miles
east of Péronne at Epéhy, and almost equally distant
from Bapaume.

The sacrifices made in these gigantic battles
measured hundreds of thousands of men. The
Germans were fighting the greatest rear-guard
battle of all history with a tenacity and courage
which astonish the historian of the events. " *Marchez aux canons !* " cried Marshal Foch. But
to reach the guns, in their serried ranks, Division
after Division must first penetrate the storm of
steel presented by thousands of machine guns in
concrete emplacements, sweeping every inch of
ground and covering every blade of cover.

The price of victory is written in the cemeteries
and memorials which rear themselves from nearly
every field and copse and village amid the now
placid peace of Picardy.

The city of Amiens is the very pivot of the Somme
battlefield. The name of Amiens recalls the Peace
of 1802, between England and France, a peace not
of very long duration. The Cathedral, commenced
in 1220, to which century the main building is due,
was not completed until the end of the thirteenth
century, and it is the most complete and perfect
specimen of its age. The Cathedral is the largest
church in the world except the Church of Sophia

at Constantinople and the Cathedral of Cologne, and in height is 422 feet above the pavement, being only surpassed in France by that of Beauvais. The vast arches rise to nearly half as high, then comes a beautiful band of foliage, and the triforium upon which magnificent windows occupy the whole of the upper surface of the walls. But each feature of the Cathedral is indeed a masterpiece, whether architectural or sculptural.

Heaven knows how the windows survived the bombardment of Amiens in 1918, when the mediæval glories of Ypres had already been pulverized beyond any kind of recognition. No detail within the Cathedral is more exquisite than the choir with its one hundred and ten magnificent stalls, executed between 1508 and 1522 by four Amienoise artists, one of whom, Jean Turpin, has signed his name on the eighty-sixth stall on the left. Of the choir Ruskin has written :

> Under the carver's hand the wood seems to cut like clay, to fold like silk, to grow like living branches, to leap like living flame. Canopy crowning canopy, pinnacle piercing pinnacle—it shoots and wreathes itself into an enchanted glade, inextricable, imperishable, fuller of leafage than any forest, and fuller of story than any book.

The quiet villages of the Somme battlefields are possessed of high historical interest, though so much of that which had endured through centuries was destroyed within a few swift days of modern warfare. Galignani's rather amusing *Traveller's Guide Through France*, published in 1827, notes several places which became famous during the War, and they were "Posts." The travels were by post. He notes the cambric and lace trade of Péronne, for which all Picardy has always been justly celebrated. "Péronne is defended by good fortifications and marshy environs;" and so we found it. The Germans made the fullest use of the bastions of Mont St. Quentin which towers over the town; and until the retirement of the Hindenburg Line in October, 1918, Péronne remained impregnable. Formerly Péronne was one of the most interesting places in Picardy, a very ancient city, where the early kings had a palace, which was given by Clovis II to the mayor, Erchinoald, who built a monastery here for Scottish monks under the rule of St. Fursy.

Péronne had been entered by the 48th South Midland Division, without resistance, when the Germans withdrew their line to the town of St. Quentin. But in March, 1918, it was left to the Scottish 9th Division to fight for the bones, not perhaps of their forefathers, for monks are celibates, but for those who had helped to found the world's most enduring alliance, that of Scotland and France. But they were overwhelmed, and the Germans were greatly elated by the recapture of this ancient fortress. Péronne fell finally to British arms in the notable assault by the Australians at the end of August, 1918.

Galignani takes the traveller through Cambrai, where he found much of interest, noting that formerly there existed in the city a convent of English nuns. Cambrai was captured in 1595 by the Spaniards, who remained masters of it until 1667. Throughout Picardy there are a number of

Spanish farms, built of solid masonry, which for hundreds of years have withstood the elements and provided shelter even against heavy shell-fire.

The village of Ham on the Somme, which witnessed furious fighting, and where especially enormous quantities of stores fell into the hands of the Germans in March, 1918, was rich in romance and historic association. Those who saw the enormous bastions of the château, some thirty feet thick, will remember how they wondered if such walls would remain proof to modern bombardment. Even these, with the rest of the village, were crumbled almost beyond recognition. The château, which frequently served as a prison, had included among its inmates Jeanne d'Arc; Condé, the Huguenot leader; Riom, the lover of the Duchesse de Berri, daughter of the Regent; a vast number of victims of the Revolution; the Ministers of the *coup d'état* of 1830; and Prince Louis Napoleon in 1840 when he was captured in an abortive attempt to regain the throne of France. The Prince remained at Ham for more than five years, and devoted himself steadily to study. " History, politics, mechanics, physics, chemistry, all had their turn; and in after-years he used to speak of having studied at the University of Ham." [1] It was a University which he, not unnaturally, wished to quit; and in May, 1846, when a number of workmen were busy with repairs, he dressed like a joiner, shaved his moustache, shouldered a plank and walked past the sentry, out through the gate, whence he escaped to England.

[1] *Edinburgh Review*, " The Bonapartes."

Quite close is the village of Villers Bretonneux, where the Australians covered themselves with imperishable glory and held the gates of Amiens. The village was also the scene of the first battle between the French and the Prussians of the north in November, 1870.

The Australian counter-attack at Villers Breton-neux, where stands the Australian Memorial, over-shadows other feats of arms by " the Diggers." But no corner of France was so thickly sown with Australian dead as the summit of the ridge between Pozières and Mouquet Farm beside the Albert–Bapaume Road. The Australian War Memorial Board in 1935 purchased the plot of land on which previously had stood the famous Windmill at Pozières. Fenced in, the inscription reads, " The ruin of Pozières windmill, which lies here, was the centre of the struggle on this part of the Somme battlefield in July and August, 1916. It was captured on August 4 by Australian troops, who fell more thickly on this ridge than on any other battlefield of the war." Gallipoli is, of course, Australia's most sacred acre, but the Pozières site in Picardy possesses memories as rich as those associated with the historic epic of Villers Bretonneux.

CHAPTER III

HIGH WOOD—SOMME

Amiens, the focus—Tactical importance of High Wood—Mametz—Albert
—The National Road—All ways lead to High Wood—The Memorials
—Eye-witness account of the first attack—" Greek meets Greek "—
The Wood as it is.

THE town of Amiens is the focus point for the Somme
battlefield. A busy little city, with its cafés, open-
fronted in the summer months, lining the main
street, a market town for the rich pastures and arable
lands—and how enriched by blood !—of great farms
which lie to the east. Amiens Cathedral, so hugely
sandbagged during the War, remains as it has for
centuries, a sublime example of Gothic architecture.
Nothing more beautiful has been conceived by man
than the jewelled windows which at certain hours
diffuse the sun's rays in the kaleidoscopic colours
illumining the slender pillars and arches which
support the trellised roof of this noble edifice. The
interior has been enriched by memorials to the
Fallen, erected beside the bronze and stone effigies
of other saints of a bygone age.

It is not difficult to conjure from the imagination a
picture of the great platform of Amiens Station,
thronged with British troops. For so it was. By
day and night, thousands of men, their uniforms
streaked with chalk and smeared with mud, their
faces and hands grimed, nothing clean about them
except the shining steel of the arms which they
carried, sat and lay huddled on the platforms,
exhausted almost beyond endurance by battle, until
the leave trains should carry their weary bodies
beyond the threat of gun-fire. And others would be

returning, lingering for a last moment of release in the streets of Amiens before returning to the hideous plague spots of the Somme, from which it seemed improbable they would ever return again. Nor is this any over-statement, for of those mobilized by the British Army for military service of all kinds, nearly one-third became casualties, excluding the ravages of disease. When there have been eliminated the vast number of non-combatants and all those employed in services outside the range of fire, and when it is realized that the ratio of deaths to wounded was in the proportion of two to five, and having regard to the unparalleled ferocity of the fighting throughout on the Somme battlefields, it is no exaggeration to say that the chance between life and death for any one of those who participated in the daily struggle was never more than an equal one.

The miracle is that men survived, and that some even who participated in all the battles of the three main phases of the conflict went through unscathed. But the cemeteries which tell of the dead and of the immense numbers of missing, whose memory is enshrined in the memorials, speak with eloquence of the tremendous sacrifices made by men, no matter of what race, in the agony of the Somme. Think of Amiens gay with laughter, its streets filled with men on leave from death, spending money upon foolish trifles, and sometimes yielding to temptations, the fruitful satisfaction of which some other ordered life appeared to suggest as being remote beyond imagination.

High Wood (Bois de Foureaux), between Martin-puich and Longueval, because of its eminence and

E

supreme tactical position, overshadows the tale of
the fight for possession of other woods and copses
within this area. Of them all, Mametz Wood is the
largest in the Somme area. Thick with trees and
undergrowth, in high summer its thickets were
steeped in gloom, and it held terrors untold. The
Welsh, more than all others, fought for mastery of
this Wood, behind whose every tree there lurked a
sniper, and from which, honeycombed with dug-outs,
there sprang machine gunners. Even long after
the wood had been secured, a German artillery
officer remained at his post in a dug-out to which was
connected a telephone, directing the fire of his guns
upon those who surged up the road of the " Valley
of Death." Never will Mametz Wood yield its
story, and for ever, amid its tangled scrub and fallen
trees, will remain the bones of the missing.

The main route to the centre of the battlefield
follows the National Road through Querrieu to
Albert, a city entirely rebuilt from the ruins of the
War. It was at Querrieu in the Château, preserving
a quiet dignity before the park lands which front
the road, that Lord Rawlinson, commanding the
Fourth Army, had his Headquarters ; and every house
of the village was occupied by at least one member of
the Staff. Albert will always be remembered for
the great gilt figure of the Virgin Mary, which,
hurled from its pedestal crowning the dome of the
church, hung perilously for months, parallel with the
ground. Men said that when the figure fell it would
be the end of the War. But that was not so. The
church has been rebuilt as it was, and a new figure
in shining gold surmounts the city.

The story of the gilded Virgin, who again surmounts the Campanile, is interesting. Tradition
has it, coming from somewhere about the twelfth
century, that a shepherd, watching his flock near the
town, which at that time bore the name of Ancre,
while resting on his crook, stabbed the turf. A cry
from the ground came to his ear, " You wound me,
shepherd ! " and he saw that the end of his crook was
tipped with blood. The spot was inspected : unearthed from the ground there appeared a statue of
Our Lady with the Holy Child, which since then has
been reverenced as " Notre Dame de Brebieres."

Years later a huge church arose in Albert in her
veneration ; and what was known as the Pilgrimage
Church, familiar to soldiers on the Western Front,
was erected in 1885, nearly the whole of the enormous
expense being met from the small contributions of
a pious peasantry. Almost every brick is inscribed
with the name of the donor. The gilt-bronze figure
of the Virgin Mary on the summit of the church was
struck by a shell on the 15th July, 1915. Under
cover of darkness French soldiers climbed the spire
and secured the gilt figure by a steel hawser, so that it
remained, thrown out almost at right angles hanging
over the town ; and then in March, 1918, the figure
fell to defeat the superstition of the time.

The road from Albert leads straight on to " The
Wood." The hard-fought woods of the Somme
battlefield include those of Mametz, Fricourt, Bazentin, Delville, Thiepval, Foureaux, Trones, St. Pierre
Vaast and Gommecourt. But if you speak of " The
Wood " to those who fought in the First Battle of
the Somme, it always means Le Bois de Foureaux

or, as it was known, " High Wood." For this wood crowns the summit of the main line of German defence which runs through the Flers ridge to Thiepval, and which, although but a few hundred feet in height, dominates the whole countryside for miles around. High Wood commands Albert, Corbie and Bray, as well as all those villages which nestle in the vales and every road which leads to the east. The main road from Amiens runs straight, in a series of great bounds, over the intervening downs and valleys, the back of each ridge being just a little higher than that which preceded it, so that, except in full summer, when the trees which flank the route on both sides are in full leaf, the users of the road can be seen for miles ahead as they top each rise. From the day upon which the battle opened, always upon this road, there could be seen vast columns, like an endless moving frieze, or a river flowing, ever different and continuous, as it passed the fixed scenery on its banks.

Through dust and heat and a myriad flies, the sweating Divisions traced their way along this road and others which are similar, leading through Corbie to Bercordel-Bécourt and Bray to the battle line. Hugging the sides of the roads to let pass the endless traffic of ambulances, horses, lorries, prisoners of war, water-carts, walking wounded, limbers, despatch riders, food and fodder waggons which poured ceaselessly from the forward areas, the columns of infantry and artillery stumbled and jostled forward, while exchanging familiar jests and often curses with those who passed down the valleys. The foul stench of trench sanitation and the nauseating reek of blood mingled with gas from the carnage of the shattered defences of the German front lines held the air. And even yet there are some places, like High Wood, wherein the war upheaval was so immense that this curious reek, indescribable yet unerring in its definition, smites the nostrils with its awesome familiarity.

As when the battle had expended its furies, and the incredible labour of trench warfare recommenced, as it did after colossal casualties in the attempt to master the Flers Line, so, if just before sunset you stand in the silence beside High Wood and listen, you hear the rumble of farm carts and waggons upon the roads ; and they recall precisely the same sound which limbers of food supplies, even the mails, brought to the ears of those in the outward defences and strongholds for attack, in that brief hour of lull and almost of silence, mutually acknowledged, which gave respite from gun-fire and from the death grip. "Live and let live," even in war. This was the unwritten law of trench warfare on both sides, that warriors might be fed, and to prevent retaliation.

All ways seemed to lead to High Wood. From the 14th July until winter with its bitterness eclipsed the agony of the swaying fight, this eminence could be observed from almost every part of the battle-field, wreathed in smoke. The trees, in whose leafed branches frequently were secreted German snipers, became gaunt blackened pillars, pitted with shrapnel and bullets. But from Courcelette, from Bazentin and away south beyond Guinchy and Guillemont, these sentinels could be seen holding fast to the ridge. And it was not until September 25th, when the first Tanks ground timbers and trenches and bodies among the roots, that High Wood passed wholly into our hands. So, if the traveller follows the road from Amiens to Courcelette,[1] and then turns aside down the lane which runs to the village of Martinpuich, and proceeding south for a bare mile halts beside the Wood, he will receive with dramatic force an impression of the strength of the German position. And if he goes into the Wood, he will find yet standing the forlorn and smitten stumps of trees, into some of which an undefeatable Nature has imparted her strength, and from these corpses has thrown out fresh shoots and lower branches; while from the lattice-work of roots there have sprung up young saplings to inherit the history of High Wood. Passing through High Wood in August, 1934, I found trunks of trees, one of them at the eastern corner, so familiar, standing, pitted with shrapnel and machine-gun bullets. And everywhere throughout the Wood, scarcely concealed by undergrowth, were steel helmets, rifle barrels, quantities of bombs, boots, and the remains of all kinds of equipment.

Immediately beside the Wood now stand the Memorials to the 47th London Division, and to the First Battalions of both the Black Watch and the Cameron Highlanders. The area of the fighting for High Wood, for whose possession the struggle continued for more than ten weeks of violent fighting, within the narrow triangle formed by Ovillers, Courcelette and Delville Wood, covers a depth from

[1] At the Café on the cross-roads kept by the Marquant family, offering good fare to the traveller.

the German front line to the Wood of less than five miles. Within this narrow space, occupied by three or four hamlets, copses and downs, now under root crops, cereals and grass upon which graze sleek cattle, hundreds of thousands of lives, British and German, were snatched during the battles between July, 1916, and September, 1918. These fields were literally soaked with blood. But it was the first battle of 1916 which demanded by far the highest price.

The main line of the first attack against High Wood pursued its way through Fricourt, up past Mametz to Bazentin, and then across the intervening valley up to High Wood. That road, under continuous shell-fire and soaked with gas, was known as the Valley of Death. Turning south, just short of where the farms of Bazentin stand amid a clump of trees upon a hillock, there is a lane cut deeply through the hillside, which was known as Caterpillar Valley; and in this shelter British and Indian cavalry were held in reserve for the break-through expected as the result of the attack on the 15th July. Two squadrons of cavalry were flung into the battle on the late afternoon of this date, and despatches issued gave the world to believe that, although since the early days of 1914 there had been no cavalry action, victory had come to British armies, and the hounds of war had been let loose upon a flying enemy. These squadrons perished before they even reached the summit on which stands High Wood.

Within this once-smitten area there are more than twenty cemeteries; and Memorials to the South Africans, whose Brigade almost perished in the carnage of Delville Wood; to the King's Royal

Rifle Corps, the famous 60th, whose Roll of Honour includes the great battles of the Peninsular War, of China, South Africa, Egypt and India, and which marches beneath the inspiring motto of " Celer et audax." Other Memorials are to the 1st Australian Division ; to the Tank Corps, for against High Wood was the first action of these awe-inspiring engines of war ; and there are cemeteries which especially commemorate the men of Norfolk and of Canada. Separate Memorials have been set up to the 35th Division, known as the Bantams, because it was formed of men too short of stature to take their place among those of larger build ; and to the men of " Tyneside," the 34th Division.

Of the Memorials, which are something more than testimonies to immortal sacrifice, those of the 47th Division in Martinpuich, and that of Canada but a short mile away on the main road near Courcelette, are contributions especially worthy. To Martin-puich, the City of London gave its school and *Mairie*, built in solid stone, with a wide forecourt which serves as a playground, and to which entry is obtained through a noble archway upon which are inscribed the Battle Honours of the London Division. The Canadian Memorial takes the form of a garden, fashioned from a wide variety of flowering shrubs, and the wide flagged paths are flanked by Canadian maples. Seats of massive stone and a low centre-piece, hewn from gigantic blocks of granite, furnish this garden as a centre for rest and meditation.

In order to provide an enduring impression of the experiences of those who fought for High Wood, I contribute hereunder my own account as an eye-

witness who took part in the first main assault upon
the Wood itself.

At the head of a Company of machine-gunners,
weary, my body soaked with sweat, face thick with
dust and streaked with lines from perspiration
which poured from beneath a steel helmet, I plodded
forward. My spirits were high: I had girded my
loins for the attack; and I think that something of
the spirit of martyrs now dwelt in my soul.

The column crossed the German trench system
early on the 14th July.

Up through the ruins of Montauban, where the
enemy still grinned in his ghastly sleep, the Division
wound its way along the pitted road. My eyes
swept the bitter landscape, from a corner of which
the shattered wooden crosses, in ragged disorder,
beckoned to my disciplined and orderly spirit. The
squat stump of an old fruit tree on the edge of a
cemetery, stripped of its leaves, curiously reminded
me of a friendly veteran in the garden at home.

My Company was tried, had been refined. Sure.
Sure as God made little apples . . . and here and
everywhere death stalked. There would be no
ripened fruit in the autumn. How many of the
men who bravely stepped behind me would return?
How many in the presence of physical death were
ready to put off this mortal body, as part of a whole-
sale massacre, limbs hurled hideously to the four
winds, or crushed in the shambles of a dug-out?
How many realized the fullness of spiritual life?

I think I could read the thoughts of these un-
tutored lads. The full tragedy of modern warfare
was laid bare to the eyes of some for the first time.

The ribaldry tossed from mouth to mouth was the camouflage for fresh horrors, which nearly every step revealed. The bloated carcasses of animals with distended stomachs lay in every ditch; and each bend of the road multiplied the bodies mutilated beyond recognition, distorted from almost any semblance of human form, lying everywhere unburied. Poor little apples: fear was in many hearts, fear of the unknown. The air reverberated with the thunder of bombardment. Great shells hurled themselves through the trees shorn of their summer splendour, torn and jagged, and buried themselves beneath the undergrowth of Mametz Wood, hard by the bitter road. A burnt-out ambulance and abandoned stretchers, soaked with blood now clotted brown and fly-blown, piled themselves beside lines and groups of English soldiers, who had perished before the murderous fire of machine guns, which for long hours had seemed riveted to the corners of the Wood.

As the road met Caterpillar Valley, above which stood the lone tree mocking both sides of the battlefield, chalk-whitened guides cowered beside deep dug-outs cut from the banks of the sunken road.

My Company passed up the gentle slope to Bazentin, lying bleak, its shattered walls, gaunt, pink-dusted ruins echoing with the unceasing chatter of machine-gun fire, and wound its way through woods in which wild strawberries still held their sweet greeting for the passer-by : while a fitful bombardment plunged indiscriminate shell-fire among the clattering bricks, from the midst of which a splintered crucifix reared itself as the symbol of sacrifice.

It was noon. The Company spread itself in a ditch from which across the valley through the dust and haze of the British bombardment could be seen the leafy trees of High Wood, to the left flank the village of Martinpuich with its halo of pink brick-dust, and to the south, Delville Wood, sprawling upon the hillside. And beside the wood, Waterlot Farm, the name familiar in all Flanders.

A runner, great beads of sweat on his brow, fear in his eyes, brought a message for me to report at Brigade Headquarters installed in a deep dug-out, cut from the chalk of the hillside.

The valley had been filled with tear-gas. Men, presenting the appearance of hideous pantomime figures from a Tibetan passion play, groped with monstrous nose- and eye-pieces. I, dragging my feet through rifles, coils of wire, boxes of bombs, and those mechanical contraptions which are the panoply of war, with smarting blood-seared eyes, joined the group of Battalion Commanders behind the blanket curtain. My Brigadier explained briefly that the Battalion deploying in the valley east of Bazentin, with the whole Division, was to attack at 9.30 the following morning. The objective was firstly High Wood and Martinpuich, and thence an unlimited field of advance through the city of Bapaume. The deployment ground was to be reconnoitred during the evening.

I returned to the Company little better informed, but with a map, well marked with arrows pointing to the east. An unfortunate shell, during my absence, had killed one and wounded three men, one of whom I met upon the pathway, happy with

men from other units with their " Blighty ones."
Late in the afternoon, with my section commanders,
I passed along the narrow road leading down to the
valley, at the higher end of which, now wreathed in
smoke, stood High Wood.   For a few minutes I conversed with a Major of Indian Horse, and learned

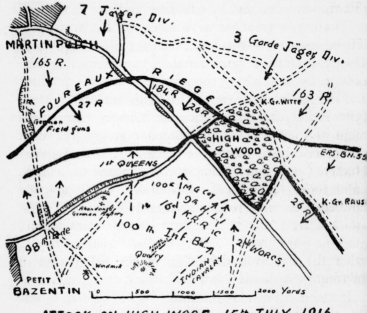

ATTACK ON HIGH WOOD, 15ᵗʰ JULY, 1916.
(FOUREAUX - WALD)

that the Cavalry were concentrating in Caterpillar
Valley and would break through so soon as High
Wood was captured, and this, the last line of German
defence, had been pierced.

The British Artillery still continued its hurricane
fire upon the wood, while observation officers
directed it from vantage-points in Bazentin.   On

my return, having viewed the ground for deployment, I questioned a gunner as to the enemy's
disposition and strength. "It's a cake-walk," replied the gunner. "Nothing can live there, my
dear fellow, nothing can live there!"

During the night, patrols went out to make contact with the enemy. They were fired upon from
the Wood's edge and by riflemen lying out in scoops
and in narrow trenches west and south of the village.
They discovered that the Germans had laid out
several strands of wire, uncut by the Artillery, and,
hidden by the long grass, forming a considerable
and dangerous obstacle. The Brigadier was wrath-
ful: repeatedly he requested a further bombardment, but such requests were made in vain or were
not practicable. He fumed with anger, cursed the
Higher Command through the bristles of a red
moustache. As a sound tactician he was not unfamiliar with the results to Infantry of a frontal
attack against uncut wire, enfiladed by well-posted
machine guns.

"P.B.I.," I reflected, a sobriquet, so truthful:
an Infantry so soused in blood.

In the early morning, under cover of a thick mist,
the 100th Brigade was deployed in the valley some
eight hundred yards west of High Wood. A heavy
dew was on the ground and hung like pearls upon
each blade of grass. After the turmoil of the preceding night an eerie stillness pervaded the atmosphere. No shot was heard, except a faint echo
from the flank.

Men spoke in whispers. Their faces were pallid,
dirty, and unshaven, many with eyes ringed with

fatigue after the night, hot and fœtid, gaseous and disturbed by shell-fire, in Bazentin. Few there were whose demeanour expressed eagerness for the assault. They were moving into position with good discipline, yet listless, as if facing the inevitable. Their identity as individuals seemed to be swallowed up in the immensity of war : devitalized electrons. I, with my Company, was deployed behind the Glasgow Highlanders, which with the 16th King's Royal Rifles was to lead the assault upon the Wood. By 8.30 a.m. the Brigade had deployed into position and lay down in the long grass awaiting the signal to assault, timed for an hour later.

I passed the time with dried blades of grass, chivvying the red ants and preventing them from crossing a narrow trench which I had scratched with a finger-nail. And I pencilled a sketch or two. It was restful and pleasant lying in the warm humid atmosphere, belly to the ground, in the quiet of the early morning.

I looked up suddenly. The mist was clearing, rising rapidly. The sun peered through, orange and round, topping the trees of High Wood. Then its rays burst through the disappearing mists, and all the landscape, hitherto opaque and flat, assumed its stereoscopic vivid form. The Wood seemed quite near, just above us up the hillside ; a little to the left behind a broken hedge was an abandoned German battery, dead gunners and horses around it. The village of Martinpuich, jagged ruins and rafters all askew, broken walls and shattered fruit trees, looked down. Both trees and village appeared Gargantuan, and the men waiting to attack like midgets from Lilliput. From my cover I scanned the landscape. Not a shot was fired. The men crouching in the grass must be visible to watchful observers in the Wood, but all remained quiet. I glanced down at my watch. Ten minutes to go: the attack was timed for 9.30.

I could see the broad kilted buttocks and bronzed thighs and knees of the 9th H.L.I. lining the slope ahead of me. They were lying in regular lines. A wind seemed to stir the tall grass. My heart thumped in my throat. I raised my head as the Highlanders rose to their feet, bayonets gleaming in the morning sun. My eyes swept the valley—long lines of men, officers at their head in the half-crouching attitude which modern tactics dictate, resembling suppliants rather than the vanguard of a great offensive, were moving forward over three miles of front. As the attackers rose, white bursts of shrapnel appeared among the trees and thinly across the ridge towards Martinpuich.

For a moment the scene remained as if an Aldershot manœuvre. Two, three, possibly four seconds later an inferno of rifle and machine-gun fire broke from the edge of High Wood, from high up in its trees, and from all along the ridge to the village. The line staggered. Men fell forward limply and quietly. The hiss and crack of bullets filled the air and skimmed the long grasses. The Highlanders and riflemen increased their pace to a jog-trot. Those in reserve clove to the ground more closely.

I, looking across the valley to my left flank, could see the men of the 1st Queens passing up the slope to Martinpuich. Suddenly they wavered and a few of the foremost attempted to cross some obstacles in the grass. They were awkwardly lifting their legs over a low wire entanglement. Some two hundred men, their Commander at their head, had been brought to a standstill at this point. A scythe seemed to cut their feet from under them, and the line crumpled and fell, stricken by machine-gun fire. Those in support wavered, then turned to fly. There was no shred of cover and they fell in their tracks as rabbits fall at a shooting battue.

Up the slope before me, the line of attack had been thinned now to a few men, who from time to time raised themselves and bounded forward with leaps and rushes. I could see men in the trees taking deliberate aim down upon those who still continued to fight, or who in their scores lay dead and wounded on the hillside.

My orders were to move forward in close support of the advancing waves of Infantry. I called to my Company, and section by section in rushes we were prepared to move forward. As we rose to our feet a hail of machine-gun bullets picked here an individual man, there two or three, and swept past us. I raised a rifle to the trees and took deliberate aim, observing my target crash through the foliage into the undergrowth beneath. On my right, an officer commanding a section had perished with all his men, with the exception of one who came running towards me, the whole of the front of his face shot away. On my left two other sections had been killed almost to a man, and I could see the tripods of the guns with legs waving in the air, and ammunition-boxes scattered among the dead.

BACK TO BILLETS

Eric Kennington.

With my runner, a young Scot, I crept forward among the dead and wounded, who wailed piteously, and came to one of my guns mounted for action, its team lying dead beside it. I seized the rear leg of the tripod and dragged the gun some yards back to where a little cover enabled me to load the belt through the feed-block. To the south of the Wood, Germans could be seen, silhouetted against the sky-line, moving forward. I fired at them and watched them fall, chuckling with joy at the technical efficiency of the machine. Then I turned the gun, and, as with a hose in a garden, sprayed the tree-tops with lead.

The attack of the Rifles and Highlanders had failed; and of my own Company but a few remained. My watch showed that by now it was scarcely ten o'clock. I hurriedly wrote a message reporting the position and that of the attack for the Colonel of the 2nd Worcestershires, a gallant soldier and good friend, who was in a sunken road with his Battalion in reserve three hundred yards to the rear. I gave this to my runner.

"Keep low," I said, "and go like blazes," for the waving grass was being whipped by bullets, and it scarcely seemed possible that life could remain for more than a few minutes.

A new horror was added to the scene of carnage. From the valley between Pozières and Martinpuich a German field battery had been brought into action, enfilading the position. I could see the gunners distinctly. At almost point-blank range they had commenced to direct shell-fire among the wounded. The shells bit through the turf, scatter-

F

ing the white chalk, and throwing aloft limbs, clothing, and fragments of flesh. Anger, and the intensity of the fire, consumed my spirit, and, not caring for the consequences, I rose and turned my machine gun upon the battery, laughing loudly as I saw the loaders fall.

I crept forward among the Highlanders and Riflemen, spurring them to action, giving bullet for bullet, directing fire upon the machine-gun nests, whose red flashes and wisps of steam made them conspicuous targets. The shell-fire increased from both flanks, and the smooth sward became pitted and hideous, but as each shell engraved itself upon the soil, a new scoop of cover was made for the safety of a rifleman.

A Highlander, terror in his eyes, lay on his back spewing blood, the chest of his tunic stained red. I tore open the buttons and shirt. It was a clean bullet wound, and I gave words of encouragement to the man, dragging him to a shell cavity, so that in a more upright position he could regain strength after the swamping of his lungs, and then creep back to safety.

The dismal action was continued throughout the morning, German fire being directed upon any movement on the hillside. Towards noon, as my eyes searched the valley for reinforcements or for some other sign of action by those directing the battle, I descried a squadron of Indian Cavalry, dark faces under glistening helmets, galloping across the valley towards the slope. No troops could have presented a more inspiring sight than these natives of India with lance and sword, tearing in mad caval-

cade on to the skyline. A few disappeared over it:
they never came back. The remainder became the
target of every gun and rifle. Turning their horses'
heads, with shrill cries, these masters of horseman-
ship galloped through a hell of fire, lifting their
mounts lightly over yawning shell-holes; turning
and twisting through the barrage of great shells:
the ranks thinned, not a man escaped. Months
later the wail of the dying was re-echoed among the
Himalayan foothills . . . " weeping for her children
and would not be comforted."

I realized the utter futility of any further attempt
to advance, and bent my energies to extricating such
men as remained alive and unwounded from the
battleground, now the point of concentration of gun
and machine-gun fire, upon which it was suicide
to remain. During the advance I had noted a small
chalk quarry, screened by a low hedge. My runner
rejoined me with another youngster, and together
we dismantled the machine gun and, after passing
the word among those few who survived, for with-
drawal, with my sergeant, who laid strong hands on
the ammunition boxes, we commenced the retirement to this position of better advantage.

Half-way down the slope a shell burst almost at
our feet, tearing the tripod from my hands and
throwing me face downwards. I rose immediately
through the smoke. The lad, still clasping the gun
to his side, both legs shattered and a stream of
blood pouring from under his helmet, lay uncon-
scious. We carried the broken body into the quarry.
Tenderly we stripped the wounded lad's jacket, and
cut away the blood-stained trouser-ends and puttees,

removing the boots. We bound the broken legs with first-aid dressings and made tight tourniquets above the knees to prevent further loss of blood. The lad had served with me since the formation of the Company and had always been interesting. He was a dreamer and used to sit on the edge of my dug-out at La Bassée and tell me of his dreams. The lad was half-way to Heaven; and though he had purged his soul for a celestial life, he was as good a gunner as ever I experienced.

"It's a miracle if 'e lives," said the sergeant. "Those legs are pulp : they'll 'ave to come off."

Many minutes passed, then the lad shuddered a little and opened his eyes. He winced, as in his recovering consciousness he sought to move, and the pang of pain shot through his body. Tears flooded his eyes as he realized his impotence.

"Hutchy," he whispered, one of those rare occasions in soldiering days in which a man addressed me by the familiar name by which I was known by the rank and file, " is it bad ? "

I bent my ear to the strained words. " A smack in the legs, that's all, kid. Just stick it," I replied. " Then we'll be able to get you down the line."

The wounded man smiled around him at the familiar faces, then closed his eyes.

There was nothing to do but wait.

Once I gazed across the edge of the quarry. Great shells plunged continuously upon the slope before me, the ceaseless rattle of musketry reverberated against the hillside, and echoed among the ruins of Bazentin. Martinpuich and the Wood were wreathed in smoke, shrouded in columns of dust. The stench of blood and gas pervaded the hot atmosphere : it sickened the throat and caught the lungs tightly.

Death had cut swiftly with his scythe, and now his foul breath fanned the nostrils with the nauseating reek of blood, he winked his eye from aloft with each burst of shrapnel, and his harsh laugh chattered from the mouths of a score of machine guns.

Half an hour passed, then the wounded lad re-opened his eyes. The brightness in them had departed.

" Give me some water," he panted.

I pressed his emptying bottle to the lips, placing my arm around his shoulders. I was all too familiar with the look, in which the brightness of vitality was disappearing with the pallor which robbed the skin of its warm texture.

I pressed my forefinger to the pulse : its beats were slow.

Around the quarry the turmoil heightened in its fury. The ground heaved and shuddered : great tufts of earth were hurled through the air. The descending metal bore down upon the dead and wounded, grinding battered bodies to pulp, or throwing dismembered limbs high in the air.

The lad's face paled, his lips went blue, and a troubled look came for a moment into his eyes ; then they brightened, an expression of ecstasy lighting the face. A shiver passed through the wounded man's body. For a moment he clung tightly to me, then the whole body relaxed. I glanced down quickly. Death looked from the eyes of a machine-gunner but a smile lay on the blood-flecked lips.

The fall of shells had suddenly ceased on our immediate front. As the area previously had been a maelstrom of explosives, so now, except for wisps of smoke hovering above the shell-holes, and bitter cries of the few wounded who still miraculously had survived the bombardment and now whimpered piteously for aid, or screamed in delirium and with hysteria, all was calm.

" Tighten up your belts, lads," I ordered. " We're going to advance in short bounds. After the first rush, take cover beside a casualty. Fill up with his ammunition and iron rations. I'll give you a few minutes for that . . . then on. We are going for the Wood. Between each rush take good cover . . . are you ready ? . . . right, come on ! "

Forty-one men, remnants of three regiments, rushed over the lip of the quarry and ran swiftly forward through the long dried grass. Not a shot greeted us. I, disciplined warrior, every sense alert, threw myself beside the equipment which still clung intact to the torso of a Highlander, stripped almost naked and splashed with the blood which had poured from the distorted figure. I snatched the clips of ammunition, thrusting them into my pouches, and ransacked the haversack for rations. The water-bottle had been pierced and drained. With the aid of elbows and toes I wriggled forward to another figure lying face down to the ground, unslung the water-bottle, hot in the blazing sun, and added it to my equipment. I glanced round me : some men were ready, crouching like cats, heads sunk in cover behind the dead or in shell-pits, others completing their task. I raised my head slowly and viewed the Wood. The storm of battle, shrapnel, machine-gun and rifle-fire still raged on either flank.

The tree-tops of the Bois de Foureaux, once safe harbour for pigeons, giving shade to peasant lovers, now the High Wood of battle, murder and of sudden death, hung as crazy scarecrows, their broken branches waving in mockery. They assumed fantastic human form, buffoons on stilts, the leaves, at the twig ends, a feathery motley with which to crown man's vengeance upon Nature at the zenith of her summer glory. From a birch hung the limp body of a too daring sniper, the beheaded trunk like a flour sack caught in the fork of a branch, while blood had poured down the silver surface of its trunk, whereon it had silted, black and obscene. I offered a prayer and a curse, brief, the gasp of an overwrought soul, for my little band of followers.

Then I rose. With a swift rush we swept forward, the softness of bodies yielding to our step. A wounded man called to me, his plaintive wail tearing the heart. I dammed the source of my compassion, and set myself to the purpose of the moment, then again dropped for cover and rest. No shot was fired. A third rush. The party on its narrow front in a thin irregular line was within forty yards of the Wood's edge. I whispered the words to left and to right, " Fix bayonets." Once more my lads rose from the blood-soaked fields in a mad rush. . . .

I glanced about me, a stick-bomb in hand. Three Germans lay awry and huddled at my feet, and my men were now extended in a narrow trench a few yards within the Wood. Other Germans stood to a flank, making overtures of surrender, and then came forward. Someone threw a bomb, then others. The Germans fell spattered with blood, lacerated and hideous. The bloodthirsty battle fury in me died down as I wiped the sweat from my eyes.

I dropped for cover as a German stick-bomb sped through the tree stumps. German shells were falling anew in the valley to the rear. Behind Bazentin the sun was sinking in a blood-red sky, a fitting epitaph to its day.

Each fold of ground remains. The slight quarry, in which remnants of the Brigade clustered, lies in the field, half-way down the slope between the Wood and the valley. The hedgerow, standing on a bank on the left flank of the attack, in the shelter of which the German field gun fought the Infantry attack at almost point-blank range remains as it was. Root crops and ploughed fields surrounding the cemetery show plainly where superb battalions, line after line of men, were mown down by the machine guns secreted in the defences of the Wood. No head-stone commemorates many of the men who were stricken in this first battle and in the days of hand-to-hand struggle which followed through the remaining weeks of July and up till the end of August. They lay where they fell, subsequently pulverized beyond any hope of recognition.

The front defences of High Wood, known as the Foureaux Riegel, were held by the 134th German Infantry Regiment from Saxony,[1] and by the 93rd

[1] It is not unworthy that the Regimental Adjutant, who saw me and I him, with whom I exchanged shots at close range, has become since one of my dearest friends.

Anhalt Regiment. Strange indeed was this fact, for against that part of the line held by the German 93rd, the British 93rd, the " Thin Red Line " of history, 2nd Battalion Argyll and Sutherland High-landers, thrust the attack. When Greek meets Greek! And thrice during the War, by some astonishing coincidence, these two Regiments met one another in hand-to-hand conflict, at Loos 1915, at High Wood and in the Battle of the Menin Road in September, 1917, within one day exactly of the same date as that upon which they had faced one another in 1915.

Mountains of rusted metal, even twenty years later, have been gathered in every village, as the plough has turned fragments of shell, rifle barrels, bayonets, and the accessories of the War ; and so no doubt it will continue for years to come. For thousands of tons of metal have been plunged into the soil. As one stands and glances across this landscape of woods and downs, hamlets and rows of tall trees lining the roads, irresistibly, the master pictures of Corot, of Daubigny and of Delacroix spring to the mind. But it is at sunset, and especially in winter, when the trees are shorn of their leaves, that the landscape seems to give back something of the atmosphere which held it when those fields were the scene of battle, murder and of sudden death.

And early on a summer morning there is often the same kind of mist, hanging low in the valley below Bazentin, which, as if lifted by some unseen agency, floats away like gossamer, leaving the golden and emerald splendour of the young trees bathed in sunshine. It was on just such a morning that the British Brigades, filled with high hope, eager for victory, lay in the long grass at the foot of the valley awaiting the hour planned for attack. But with what bitterness they viewed the tree trunks and leafy branches of the trees of High Wood, just at the very moment when as they raised themselves to the attack the early mists were dissipated by the morning sunshine! And with what ferocity the sun burned during that day of agony whereon the dying cried for respite from its scorching rays, the wounded whimpered for water, and men fighting the battle for the Wood strove furiously and vainly with tongues cleaving to the roofs of their mouths!

CHAPTER IV

THE SOMME BATTLE-LINE, 1916

THE fulcrum of the Somme battlefield is sustained on the Flers Ridge, and the battles to the north of Albert, though perhaps not distinguished by the drama of the Wood, were no less intense, and cost Britain untold blood and treasure.

A view of the first phase of the battle can be obtained by going north as far as Foncquevillers, some ten miles to the north of Albert. This village was one of those which, although but a mile behind the front lines, by some unwritten tradition had been immune from shell-fire; and in Hébuterne, hard by, small stalls did a roaring trade long after the battle had reached the height of its fury. The trenches opposite the Park of Gommecourt were a kind of rest area, and so quiet was this front that even glass remained in the windows of Foncquevillers. The northern extremity of the British attack on 1st July, 1916, was disposed to debouch from our lines in front of Hébuterne, to wrest the Park of Gommecourt from the enemy, to squeeze out the high ground at Beaumont-Hamel, and to force the enemy to retreat beyond the valley of the River Ancre.

The story of the breakdown of the attack upon the Gommecourt front is one of the most gruesome in the annals of our military history. The attack here by the Third Army was for the purpose of

enabling the more important assault against the
Leipzig and Schwaben redoubts, which bulwarked
the Thiepval plateau and spur. The attack completely failed, destroyed by machine-gun fire.
One German Infantry Regiment alone, the 180th,
opposed the assault of ten thousand men. Opposite
to Gommecourt the lines were separated from one
another by a distance of from one to two hundred
yards only. Those comparatively few men who
succeeded in reaching the German lines found themselves unsupported, heavily bombed from both
flanks, and were finally overwhelmed by counter-
attack and were slaughtered or captured. The
ravine which lay between the lines was heaped with
dead, and there for weeks they lay, the prey of rats
and of myriads of swollen flies.

The extent of this catastrophe appears unbelievable.
Superb Battalions were reduced within a few minutes
to but skeletons of their strength ; and the ravine
remained as a grim testimony to the efficacy of the
machine gun and to the folly of frontal attacks
against machine-gun positions in the hands of a
well-entrenched enemy.

Proceeding south, Beaumont-Hamel is reached ;
and within little more than two square miles there
are more than twenty cemeteries. But the fighting
for possession of the Thiepval plateau, which also
commands Bapaume, was no less hideous than
that which was the fate both of the attack and of
the defence at High Wood. An enormous arched
memorial stands on Thiepval Ridge, at whose
dedication the Prince of Wales was present. The
casualties were perhaps the more severe in the

initial fighting because whole Divisions almost fresh from the training camps in England, beyond the first experience of trench warfare, received here their first baptism of fire. " Foolhardiness, even that is not to be despised," wrote Von Clausewitz, the great German master of military strategy. If gallantry to the point of recklessness could have won battles, then the assaults at Thiepval and Beaumont-Hamel must have been numbered among the greatest of the world's military victories, but there was no such result. Agony incredible : Battalions, Brigades, Divisions, were almost annihilated between dusk and dawn ; and those few who remained were thrust back again to the point from which they started.

In the spring of 1917, Sir William Orpen, the master painter, wandered over the Somme battle-fields and at Beaumont-Hamel penned this note :

A fair spring morning—not a living soul is near.   Far, far away there is the faint grumble of the guns ; and battle has passed long since.

All is Peace.

At times there is the faint drone of aeroplanes as they pass overhead, amber specks, high up in the blue. Occasionally there is the movement of a rat in the old battered trench on which I sit, still in the confusion in which it was hurriedly left.

The sun is baking hot.

Strange odours come from the door of a dug-out with its endless steps running down into blackness.

The land is white—dazzling.   The distance is all shimmering in heat.

A few little spring flowers have forced their way through the chalk.

He lies a few yards in front of the trench.

We are quite alone.

He makes me feel very awed, very small, very ashamed.

He has been there a long, long time—hundreds of eyes have seen him, hundreds of bodies have felt faint and sick because of him.

Then this place was Hell, but now all is Peace.

And the sun has made him Holy and Pure—he and his garments are bleached white and clean.

A daffodil is by his head, and his curly, golden hair is moving in the slight breeze.

He, the man who died in "No-Man's-Land," doing some great act of bravery for his comrades and country— here he lies, Pure and Holy, his face upward turned; no earth between him and his Maker.

I have no right to be so near.[1]

If the Muse gave words to a painter that he might set down the poignant feelings of his heart, denied in pigments even to a master of his craft, there were many others, fighting men, from whom sheer agony wrung poetry sublime.

Thy dear brown eyes which were as depths where truth
  Lay bowered with frolic joy, but yesterday
Shone with the fire of thy so guileless youth,
  Now ruthless death has dimmed and closed for aye.

Those sweet red lips, that never knew the stain
  Of angry words or harsh, or thoughts unclean,
Have sung their last gay song.   Never again
  Shall I the harvest of their laughter glean.

The goodly harvest of thy laughing mouth
  Is garnered in ; and lo ! the golden grain
Of all thy generous thoughts, which knew no drouth
  Of meanness, and thy tender words remain

Stored in my heart ; and though I may not see
  Thy peerless form nor hear thy voice again,
The memory lives of what thou wast to me,
  We knew great love. . . .   We have not lived in vain.[2]

---

[1] *An Onlooker in France*, by Sir William Orpen, K.B.E., R.A.
[2] *The Dead Soldier*, Sydney Oswald.

And with thoughts turning wistfully towards
" the Golden Valley down by Tintern on the Wye,"
at Albert on the 22nd July, 1916, another poet
wrote :

> Dust and corpses in the thistles
> Where the gas-shells burst like snow,
> And the shrapnel screams and whistles
> On the Bécourt road below,
> And the High Wood bursts and bristles
> Where the mine-clouds foul the sky . . .
> *But I'm with you up at Wyndcroft,*
> *Over Tintern on the Wye.*[1]

The Memorials to the 29th Division, fresh from
the bitter disappointment of its Gallipoli adventure ;
to the Newfoundlanders ; to the 51st Highland
Division ; to the Royal Naval Division ; to the
men of Yorks and Lancs and of Argyllshire and to
those of Ulster, tell something of the Territorial
contribution to the capture of Beaumont-Hamel
ridge. But while the offensive opposite to High
Wood was crushed into the ground and became
one of trench, of bomb and of mortar, the operations
around the valley of the Ancre for the occupation
of its heights, in August, developed into and became
known as the Battle of the Ancre, subsidiary to,
though part of, the Battle of the Somme.

Some 50,000 men leaped to the first assault before
Gommecourt and Beaumont-Hamel. It was not
until the later stages of the Ancre battle, pursuing
that of the Somme, that the latter fell into our hands.
The attack against Gommecourt was carried out by
London Territorials, while the assault upon Beaumont-Hamel was launched by " Kitchener " Bat-
alions from Yorkshire and Lancashire who assailed

---

[1] *The Iron Music*, Ford Madox Hueffer.

the Wurtemburg Division. Nothing could have excelled the valour of the German defence. A British General who surveyed the whole scene, said : " I cannot adequately express my admiration for the British who advanced or for the Germans who stood up under such a heavy barrage to oppose them." Faithful historian, the late Sir Arthur Conan Doyle, who kept the closest touch with all the operations throughout the War, wrote : " It is to the skill and to the personal gallantry of the German machine gunners that the result is to be traced." [1] The Wurtemburg machine gunners even rushed their machine guns forward in order both to escape the severity of the barrage and to enfilade the lines of the attack. " They were seen exposed waist-deep and dropping fast, but mowing the open slope as with a scythe of steel." And there were recorded instances of chivalry on the part of German officers and soldiers, both on this front and elsewhere, which tore aside the curtain of inflammatory propaganda, presenting the German soldiers as men of humane and generous sentiments no less than were the Allies.

" The great mine at La Boisselle was a wonderful sight." [2] Thus wrote the supreme painter of the War, Sir William Orpen. And he continues :

One morning I was wandering about the old battlefield and I came across a great wilderness of white chalk—not a tuft of grass, not a flower, nothing but blazing chalk apparently a hill of chalk dotted thickly all over with bits of shrapnel. I walked up to it, and suddenly found myself

---

[1] *The British Campaigns in Europe*, 1914–1918, by Arthur Conan Doyle.

[2] *An Onlooker in France*, by Sir William Orpen, K.B.E., R.A.

on the lip of the crater. I felt myself in another world. This enormous hole, 320 yards round at the top, with sides so steep one could not climb down them, was the vast, terrific work of man. Imagine burrowing all that way down in the belly of the earth, with Hell going on over-head, burrowing and listening till they got right under the German trenches—hundreds and hundreds of yards of burrowing. And here remained the result of their work, on the earth at least, if not on humanity. The latter had disappeared ; but the great chasm, with one mound in the centre at the bottom, and one skull placed on top of it, remained. They had cut little steps down one of its sides, and had cleared up all the human remains and buried them in this mound. That one mound, with the little skull on the top, at the bottom of this enormous chasm, was the greatest monument I have ever seen to the handiwork of man.

Although other mine craters impressed him—for example, that at Beaumont-Hamel and the " Cough-drop " at High Wood—there was none which could " compare in dignity and grandeur with the great mine of La Boisselle."

With a sense of history, it is impossible to leave this area and go south again without feelings of intense sadness. And along the road which follows the River Ancre back to Albert, on both sides, there are cemeteries which recall notable trenches, woods and strong points, whose names were as familiar to those who participated in the Battle of the Somme as is Piccadilly to Londoners and Princes Street to those who claim Edinburgh as their capital city. The Memorial to the Miners stands close beside Ovillers, where have been pre-served the craters of the giant mines which were exploded from subterranean galleries that wrecked the German trench system at this point. You

G

stand on the edge of the chalk crater and peer
down forty feet into its bowels; and these grim
relics recall the little-known heroism of those who
mined and countermined, hearing the tap-tap of the
opposition, mole-like, somewhere in a gallery near
by, ready to blow. And it recalls the immensity
of the mining effort beneath the famous Brick Stacks
beside the La Bassée canal, the passages and corridors
and underground dwellings of Arras and the fœtid
funk-holes of Passchendaele. And there is the
Memorial, too, to the 19th Division, once so familiar
with the sign of the butterfly upon the tail-boards of
its limbers and waggons.

The mud of the Somme battlefields was of a very
different quality from that remembered with equal
abhorrence in the Ypres sector. The mud on the
Somme sucked like a quicksand. It was sticky
as treacle: it appeared to be bottomless. The
familiar " duck tracks," long wooden laths covered
as is a bath mat, of the northern sectors were useless
on the Somme. Stand anywhere between Les
Bœufs and Rancourt, and the feet will rest on soil
into which men sank waist, even breast, deep in the
quagmire. Roads disappeared beneath the surface
of oozing mud, trenches were water-logged, a pitiless
rain descended.

The burden of movement, let alone of offensive
action, rendered the task of shifting ammunition,
stores, rations, and the ever-increasing wounded
almost impossible. And so British troops, huddled
in insecurity by day, waited for darkness during which
at least succour could be brought to the wounded
without fear of a sniper's bullet, and an effort with

ropes and stimulants could be made to free men, half drowned and frozen, held fast in the mud. Some of these, huge fellows, belonging to the Household Cavalry, dismounted, became living corpses. They had missed the line of our posts in the darkness and became stranded in No-Man's-Land, from whence they could not be rescued. Their heads could be seen and insane cries heard as they slowly perished or were put beyond further misery by a chance shell or sniper's bullet. And yet the demand was always that the attack should go forward.

From Guillemont the Guards Division, already engaged in heavy fighting, was charged with the assault on the Flers Line. Their casualties were enormous, and included the son of Mr. Herbert Asquith, the former Prime Minister. The Guards seized the stinking ruins of Les Bœufs and carried the attack at last on to the Flers Ridge, while the defence slipped back to Le Transloy. A fresh network of trenches appeared, known by such evil names as Brimstone, Hazy, Thunder, and Hurricane. The Tanks, except for their novelty and the immense publicity contributed to their first success, added little to the battle, their action at most being isolated. The Guards' Cemetery at Les Bœufs and Combles, beside the battlefield, is some indication of the enormous losses sustained by Britain's *corps d'élite*. Yet even in November the attack was pursued before the defences of Le Transloy.

It was in this last effort that the British Army joined action closely with the French. The latter in the early stages of the battle, attacking south, astride the Somme, had met with marked success and with little opposition. While the British were everywhere held, the French attack in one bound had leaped forward to the gates of Péronne. But there it too was arrested. By the middle of November the Somme battle had perished in the mud, and the British Army took over the remainder of the line from the French as far south as the Somme. The streets of Combles, which still bore some resemblance to its former self, and the slopes which led up to the village of Bouchavesnes, were strewn with the sky-blue uniforms of the French dead who had failed to take St. Pierre-Vaast Wood, and the attack failed also before the defences of Mont St. Quentin. No victory was added to the record of British military history by the results of this second phase of the Battle of the Somme. It had worn itself into a battle of attrition which probably told more severely upon the attack than upon the defence, though here opinions are divided, and perhaps it would be truer to say that the scales were evenly balanced, for in the Battle of Arras, which followed in the spring, there was no weakening in the ardour of the attack, none in the gallantry of the defence; and so it was, also, to the date of the Armistice.

Within this area there stand the Memorials to the New Zealand Division; to the 16th Irish Division, men from what is now the Irish Free State; to the 20th Light Division, composed for the most part of men from the English Shires and Counties; to the 53rd Brigade; and there are eight cemeteries. Mont St. Quentin, standing above Péronne, can be viewed from the ridge which runs through Rancourt and Sailly Sallisel. And here it was that the British line dug itself in for the severe winter which followed.

The visitor or traveller passing through the quiet, sleepy villages and small towns of Picardy will find it difficult perhaps to picture them as replicas of Aldershot, their streets alive with troops, the cobbled roads rattling with traffic. Of all such small towns, Corbie is held in most affectionate remembrance by the generation of the War. The village—and it is no more—lay for the longer period beyond gun-fire. In this quiet place, at some period during its participation in the Somme battles, every Division in the Army took its rest. And it will be remembered that, as at Verdun, the welter of slaughter of the Somme battlefield was one to which Division after Division was systematically introduced.

Men went to the blood-bath, and what remained of their formations was withdrawn to receive reinforcements and to be re-equipped before being plunged again and again. Corbie, at the apex of the triangle based on the Flers Line, knew nearly every man who served on the Somme. There was not much of the town, and its walls mostly had been splashed high with mud from the endless stream of lorries which thundered over the *pavé* of its streets. The town with its neat streets clung around the Cathedral, huge Gothic architecture, and beneath the shadow of the Cathedral stood the Café de la Poste, and the Café Alexandre, happy meeting-places. But the Cathedral, whose great pile had stood since the twelfth century, was destroyed by gun-fire in the Second Battle of the Somme when Germany overwhelmed the Fifth Army and thrust towards Paris.

Hugging the main road which turned sharply before the Cathedral was the Place, faced by the pretentious little *Mairie*. In the evening the elders would sit and gossip, while the little children gambolled at their grandparents' feet. Often enough they were waved aside, or some older man would hobble quickly to snatch a child from beneath the feet of drummers. For each evening " Retreat " was bravely played upon the Place by such Battalions as might be resting in Corbie. One might marvel at men so recently bearing stretchers on the battle-field, now proudly rolling a tattoo on great tenor and side-drums swinging by the drummers' peculiar gait.

Drummers with heads thrown back, eyes bright, drum-sticks whirling a rhythmic pattern in the air, the crash of the big drum, the swelling roll of side-drums, the gay piping of the fifes ; and ahead, with martial pride and infinite glorious swagger, the Drum-major. And the pipes of Scotland would bid for first place as the popular favourites. The swinging kilt and sporran were superb ornamental assets, always a good asset to popular esteem and affection.

It is most interesting to remember that the ancestors of the inhabitants of Corbie, five hundred years earlier, had received English soldiers. Certainly they are the descendants of those same people who witnessed the march of King Henry V of England, for very tenaciously, generation after generation, do the peasants cling to their soil. Whenever one walks behind the battle lines of the Somme there are to be discovered relics of past British campaigns in Flanders. The intrepid King Harry severed himself from his base at Harfleur; and with a thousand men-at-arms, and rather more than three thousand archers, went to beard the might of France, then assembling at Rouen. Shakespeare, with his genius for incorporating the fact of history with romance, has preserved an incident of the occupation of Corbie by British troops. The march of Henry V, concluding with its astonishing victory at Azincourt, took place between the 8th and 29th of October, 1415. Five hundred years later British soldiers who fell in Flanders were buried beside their fore-bears-in-arms.

In Shakespeare's *King Henry V*, Act III, scene v, there is " The English Camp in Picardy," founded upon Holinshed's *Chronicles* published in 1587, and upon an old play, *The Famous Victories of Henry V*. Pistol mourned the impending fate of his comrade Bardolph.

> For he hath stol'n a pax, and hanged must 'a be,
> A damned death. . .
> . . . for pax of little price.

The man was hanged in Corbie in the shadow of the same Cathedral which towers above the village of so frequent British occupation. But, just as British Generals would fight their battles, and while in rest assist the peasants to stack their corn, so King Henry exercised a meticulous care to safeguard the inhabitants through whose lands he strode.

> We give express charge, that in our marches through the country, there be nothing compelled from the villages, nothing taken but paid for, none of the French upbraided or abused in disdainful language; for when lenity and cruelty play for a kingdom, the gentler gamester is the soonest winner.

And so the British Armies, shoulder to shoulder with their French allies, fought the Battles of the Somme. Despite the disturbance to their lives, the peasants of Picardy will always remember with kindness the visits of British troops to their villages and farms.

How singular, too, it is to compare the history of the Somme battlefields of October, 1916, with that chronicled by Holinshed of the campaign of October, 1415.

> The Englishmen were brought into some distresse in this iornie, by reason of their vittels in maner spent, and no hope to get more, for the enimies had destroyed all the corne before they came. Rest could they none take, for their enimies with alarmes did ever so infest them; dailie it rained, and nightlie it freesed; of fuell there was great scarsitie, of fluxes plentie; monie enough, but wares for their relief to bestow it on had they none. Yet in this great necessitie the poore people of the countrie were not spoiled, nor aine thing taken of them without paiement, nor aine outrage or offense donne by the Englishmen, except one, which was that a soldier took a pix out of a church, for which he was apprehended, and the King not once remooved till the box was restored, and the offender strangled. The people of the countries thereabout, hearing of such zeal in him, to the maintenance of justice, ministered to his armie victuals and other necessaries, although by open proclamation so to do they were prohibited.

Over these same fields, but culminating rather upon the ground on which was fought the Third Battle of the Somme, surging east towards Valenciennes, Maubeuge and Mons, Marlborough fought his greatest battles, to which we will come ; and George II personally led his troops in the field, just as George V standing beside the craters at Ovillers watched his men pass into the smoke and dust of the battle for the Flers Ridge.

Let us go back a little from these scenes, even as British soldiers were withdrawn from the battle-line, for Rest.

The hosts of young men from Britain increased always ; and this great confluence of a new and alien population reached its greatest numbers for the First Battle of the Somme. Not a village, scarcely a farm-house between Abbeville as the apex of the far-spread front line, but was filled with British troops for several months. The personnel might change, but new customs persisted. The road from Abbeville to Amiens follows the River Somme. The countryside consists of wide chalk downs, and is curiously reminiscent of that part of Sussex which lies over the Ouse. Millions of British boots tramped this road and thousands of cavaliers followed its course from one village to another.

Far back in time British soldiers also marched along this road. As Edward III sought to pass the Somme at Pont Remy, without success, so his force failed to capture the village of Long, perched above the river on a commanding position ; and indeed this village is one of the most beautiful along the whole course of the Somme. You pass from one

gem of habitation to another, Cocquerel, Aislly,
Le Haut Clocher, where is the tallest traceried spire
among the noble churches which throughout Picardy
everywhere are found, until you reach Fontaine,
where is situated the most beautiful of all. The
church was completed in 1561, and as a specimen of
late Pointed work it is perfect.

Nearly all these churches were built at the time
when Picardy was swept by religious wars, and this
is remarkable. For in England, during the same
period, although free from strife with her riches
expanding, not one single church was erected.
The reason may be traced perhaps to the material-
istic preoccupations which Shakespeare, writing in
this self-same era, laments.

> This blessed plot, this earth, this realm, this England,
> This nurse, this teeming womb of royal kings,
> Fear'd by their breed and famous by their birth,
> Renowned for their deads as far from home,
> For Christian service and true chivalry,
> As is the sepulchre in stubborn Jewry
> Of the world's ransom, blessed Mary's Son ;
> This land of such dear souls, this dear dear land,
> Dear for her reputation through the world,
> Is now leased out, I die pronouncing it,
> Like to a tenement or pelting farm :
> England, bound in with the triumphant sea,
> Whose rocky shore beats back the envious siege
> Of watery Neptune, is now bound in with shame,
> With inky blots and rotten parchment bonds :
> That England, that was wont to conquer others,
> Hath made a shameful conquest of itself.
> Ah, would the scandal vanish with my life,
> How happy then were my ensuing death !

You go on to Longpré, whose church was burned
by the soldiers of Edward III, and little remains
of the former building. Throughout all Picardy,

among the farms can be found those which resemble
fortresses, and indeed they were. The barns are
windowless and the entry to the courtyard is through
a gateway, guarded by immense solid doors. Several
such farms became famous during the War, their
immensely thick walls affording good cover and being
impervious to anything but the heaviest shell-fire.
Of these perhaps the best known was Waterlot
farm. A descendant of this well-known Huguenot
family, famous in the public life of the City of
London, attained to fame as an etcher in the
eighteenth century, and yet another, a painter and
member of the Royal Academy,[1] produced some
of his best known pictures in Picardy, following
the tradition of Corot and Daubigny.

There are no hedges and ditches dividing the fields
as there often are in Flanders ; and the boundaries
are marked by huge iron crucifixes decorated with
gilt rays. Such crucifixes occur very frequently ;
and they often became landmarks upon the scarred
battlefields, for strangely—and it became a matter
for superstition among the troops—these crucifixes
always seemed to survive bombardment when trees
had been uprooted and farms had been levelled to
the ground. Waterlot farm was one of the old
manoirs. So literally was it disembowelled that by
the close of the year 1916 nothing remained but a
yawning crater.

The most familiar type of farm-house is that in
whose courtyard, before the front door, stands a
dunghill, filled with all manner of muck in varous
stages of decomposition, emitting a powerful aroma.

[1] Sir Ernest Waterlow, R.A., P.R.W.S.

Marching by night from the battlefields, men always knew when they had reached a billet by the smell which heralded the farm-house in whose byres and barns they were to find cover and rest for the night.

Proceeding from Longpré, the valley now begins to narrow as it reaches Airaines. Edward III here again was unfortunate, though the castle which defied him has disappeared. Lying out on the downs are other villages, the most interesting of which is that of Flixecourt with its quaint Hôtel de Ville. This village was usually the headquarters of a Division in rest. You pass by Condé-Folies, and from here all along to Amiens tens of thousands of British troops found two or three weeks' rest in succession from the mighty engagements of the Battle of the Somme. Above the village lies the famous Roman camp of L'Étoile, whose shape is even better marked than that of Pilsdon Pen in Dorset.

Many travellers to Paris by rail, following the road and villages with their eyes, suddenly see the ruins of the Cistercian Abbaye du Gard and imagine that it must be some wreckage left from the War. But this is not so. The Abbey lies just a short distance from Picquigny, where Edward IV met Louis XI of France to discuss the marriage of his daughter with the Dauphin.

King George V of England, in May 1922, also came to Picquigny. The King was received by the Bishop of Amiens, who referred to the last visit of an English King to the village and to the precautions taken for his safety. He said that an English King might now trust himself among the people of

icardy with no guard other than their respect and
ffection for him and for his Army. Tens of
housands of soldiers must have seen the old-
ashioned café with its walls hung with fishing-rods
nd decorated with stuffed birds and enormous pike.
icquigny is a sporting centre, as it is also one for
rtists.

The last village along the Somme before the battle
ne is that of Bray. During the First Battle of the
omme the houses were almost unrecognizable,
terally bathed in mud, their plastered walls
rumpled by the ever-passing heavy motor traffic
nd patched with biscuit tins and petrol cans. But
ray has been reborn and is now again a pleasant
ttle place.

The immense dug-outs, some of them thirty and
orty feet deep, splaying out into subterranean
alleries and chambers, which honeycombed the
rench systems and battery positions, are no more.
hey were filled in by armies of German prisoners
fter the Armistice. Both the French and the
ermans always constructed dug-outs bigger and
etter and safer than those of the British. The most
alued compensation for a successful attack was the
heritance of German dug-outs, equipped as they
ere with " every modern convenience." Perhaps
e most elaborate of these in the Somme area were
Fricourt and in Mametz Wood.

The French, too, were very skilful in the prepara-
on of well-timbered retreats far below ground.
hen the British took over the French sector north
the River Somme at Sailly Sallisel, Rancourt and
ouchavesnes, there was found a wonderful series

of underground homes in the Maurepas Ravine
by Combles. No doubt the system of continental
conscription had accustomed men of all kinds of
occupations to simple military engineering, which
was lacking in the new British armies. But the
making of dug-outs in France is rooted, also, deep
in history. While all trace of the War dug-out
has been lost, vast subterranean caves exist at
Picquigny, Poix and Montreuil; at Gramont, close
to Ailly le Haut-Clocher; and at Hiermont, near
Crécy; at Echeu, close to Roye; and at Bouchoir.
The largest, on a far grander scale than the British
galleries under Arras, constructed for the battle
concentration of April, 1917, are at Naours, near
Amiens. These contain thirty streets leading to
some 250 chambers, each about twenty feet square.
This underground retreat was a veritable village,
possessing three chapels, one equipped with aisles,
altars and holy-water stoups.

Antiquarian authorities have concluded that these
refuges were begun at the period of the Norman
invasion; and certainly they sheltered the inhabitants
during the English invasions. Victor Hugo wrote
of the Insurrection in La Vendée:

> From time immemorial this system of underground
> life has existed in Brittany. In all ages man has sought
> secure retreats from man; hence the lurking-places, like
> the nests of reptiles, dug out beneath the trees. The
> dated from the time of the Druids, and some of these
> vaulted chambers were as ancient as the cromlechs of the
> plains. Beneath all these merciless tramplings, the
> inhabitants determined to disappear. Each did so in
> turn; the Troglodytes to escape the Celts; the Celts the
> Romans; the Bretons the Normans; the Huguenots the

Roman Catholics; and the smugglers the excise officers—
all these fled to the woods and burrowed underground. . . .
The ground of every wood was a species of coral reef,
pierced and traversed in every direction by an unknown
network of passages, cells and galleries.

Here too is the explanation of the ancient dug-outs
of Picardy. During the Great War they were used
to shelter women and children from long-range
shell-fire and aerial bombing.

There is not any exact limit to the Somme battlefield, either north or south, though the chief interest
is centred between the river and Beaumont-Hamel
and in the heroism and sacrifice of British and
German soldiers. In Amiens Cathedral, among
other Memorials to the Fallen is one recording the
contribution of the American Army in the Battles
of the Somme; and this refers especially to the
action by the first American contingent at Montdidier on the 28th May, 1918. Brigaded with the
3rd French Army, the American Battalions assaulted
and took the village of Cantigny with a large number
of prisoners. This action marked the first turning-
point in the fortunes of the Great War in so far
as the Somme battlefield was concerned; and here,
by defying three furious German counter-attacks,
American soldiers gained their right to stand shoulder
to shoulder with their Allies.

Shortly after this battle, the veteran American
war correspondent, Frederick Palmer, advised
General Pershing that " it would be a good thing to
have a General killed "; and in his reflections he
records that few showed themselves at the front.[1]

[1] *With My Own Eyes*, by Frederick Palmer.

He continues, " But every soldier of the Army of
Potomac had seen Grant and everyone of the Army
of Northern Carolina had seen Lee. For if these
two had impressed their personalities on seventy-
five or a hundred thousand men, a Division Commander in 1918 ought to impress his personality
on twenty-five thousand."

Montdidier, standing on a height, overlooks the
river. It is named from Didier, King of the Lom-
bards, who was imprisoned here by the Emperor
Charlemagne before he was incarcerated as a monk
at Corbie. Although the kings had sometimes held
their court in the Château, it was demolished by
Philippe Auguste to prevent it falling to the English.
But Montdidier is truly famous for the life-work of
the chemist Parmentier, born in 1737, whose statue
faces the Hôtel de Ville. Parmentier was the first
to introduce the cultivation of the potato into
France ; and the opposition which he met is not
dissimilar from that which opposed Sir Ronald
Ross in his earlier efforts to stamp out the scourge
of malaria. Superstitious, ignorant and prejudiced
people suggested that the potato plant was poisonous,
that it would surely produce an epidemic of
leprosy.

In despair, Parmentier sought an audience with
Louis XVI and succeeded in winning his confidence.
As a ruse, he persuaded the French monarch to
order that soldiers should mount guard over the
potato-field. When the critics observed Royal
troops, armed to the teeth, marching around the
potato-field, they exclaimed, " How precious must

be this blue-flowered plant!" And almost immediately demands came for the seed, the highest in the land being privileged to eat potatoes. And thus it is with almost every discovery and invention. Men have always stoned the prophets!

CHAPTER V

A HONEYCOMB OF HISTORY

THE SOMME REFOUGHT—1916–18

Abbeville—Crécy—Azincourt—Tanks—Picquigny—The Fifth Army,
Second Battle, March, 1918—Gas—Canadians and Australians—
The Hindenburg Line—The great advance, 1918—Canal de St.
Quentin—German rearguard action—Malplaquet, 1709—Chivalry
—Memorials—The crossing of the Selle River—French gratitude
—Armistice.

ABBEVILLE, on the Somme, south-west of Amiens,
was also a " rest area," in which thousands of troops
were billeted.   But it was a more important hospital
centre for the seriously wounded, men who could
be extricated from the battlefield and carried thus
far, but, lest ebbing vitality gave way, no farther.
Hard by Abbeville lies the battlefield of Crécy,
north-east of the village of that name.   No Englishman can be unmoved at Crécy when he beholds the
Tower of Edward on the hill, from which Edward
III surveyed the army and suspended the great
standard of England on that memorable day.

August 20th, 1346 !   And five hundred and
seventy years later the English King, in August
also, watched his men do battle !   In Froissart's
Chronicles there is a fine detailed description of the
battle, which in some passages recalls the bitter
fighting of the Somme battles.   " There is no man,
unless he had been present, that can imagine, or
describe, truly, the confusion of that day. . . ."
But not among the English !   " The English . . .
rose undauntedly and fell into their ranks. . . .
The English continued to take aim forcibly and
vigorously. The battle was very murderous and

cruel, and many gallant deeds of arms were per-
formed which have never been known." The
tradition as marksmen has been sustained for
centuries, for the English army of 1914 were the
finest marksmen in the world. And " a heavy rain
was falling, accompanied by thunder and darkness."
Perhaps the graceful beauty of Picardy must always
weep when men do battle in her midst.

The brave King of Bohemia was slain. A
battered, weather-beaten Cross still marks the spot
where the blind monarch feel: and one may
visit Crécy Grange, where eight hundred years
ago the monks of Valloires received and tended the
wounded, as Abbeville ministered to them in 1916.
The Battle of Crécy was a bloody fray. Apart from
the skilful archers " there were many foot-soldiers
from Cornwall and Wales, who were provided with
large knives . . . and these attacked the French. . . ."
Eleven princes, eighty bannerets, twelve hundred
simple knights, and about thirty thousand men " of
other kinds " fell upon the field of Crécy.

The town of St. Pol was to Arras what the town
of Abbeville was to Amiens, or Cassel to Ypres.
Ten miles from St. Pol on the road to Boulogne is
the village of Azincourt, where on October 25th,
1415, King Henry V overwhelmed the French in a
notable victory against odds even greater than at
Crécy. The prowess of the English archers, that
same marksmanship which decimated the German
legions in 1914, again manifested itself. King
Henry's words of scorn to a knight who wished
that a thousand stout warriors lying idle that night
in England had been standing in his ranks mark

the contrast to the mind which governed Passchendaele. " I would not have a single man more,"
the King replied. " If God give us the victory, it
will be plain that we owe it to His Grace. If not,
the fewer we are, the less loss for England."

Like the heavy gunners, 500 years later, who
sped missiles greater than the weight of man, Henry's
archers " bared their arms and dressed to give fair
play to the crooked stick and the grey goose wing,"
but for which, as the rhyme runs, " England were
but a fling." The carnage was terrible ; the Con-
nétable Delalbreth, gentleman of the French Army,
with six princes and 8,400 French nobles, died
upon the field. The French lost 10,000 men,
" *presque tous gentilhommes*," and 2,000 *seigneurs*
having banners. After the Battle of Azincourt it
was said " *voulez-vous voir la France, allez à
Londres*."

In no play other than that of *King Henry V* did
Shakespeare attempt the experiment of the dramat-
ization of war. The words which Ben Jonson
addressed to his friend Michael Drayton, the arch-
patriot among English poets, on his poem " The
Ballad of Agincourt," might more justly perhaps be
applied to William Shakespeare, as they serve also
the British soldiers who fought the latest Battles of
the Somme :

> Look how we read the Spartans were inflamed
> With bold Tyrtæus' verse ; when thou art named
> So shall our English youths urge on, and cry,
> An Agincourt ! an Agincourt ! or die.

The second phase of the Battle of the Somme
was centred again at High Wood, and its drama is

heightened by the fact that it witnessed the genesis of the Tank. The fortunes of the Somme had faded. Although by September, waist and axle deep in mud, but with so generous an experiment to exploit as the Tank, at least the element of surprise with which to defeat an unbeaten enemy, this new opportunity came to salve the reputations of those whose optimism had expected the break-through in July. So these grotesque monsters, although far too few in numbers to serve the objectives for which men had hoped, churned and pounded their way over the ill-conditioned roads in which even light waggons were axle-deep in mud and arrived at Guillemont, which by this date was but brick-dust, a name on the map. Tanks were ready to take part in the new offensive.

It is a matter for amazement that the troops called upon to take part in the new battle had suffered nothing in their morale. This is not to suggest that they affected the same kind of optimism which had distinguished them early in July. The vast majority were survivors of the earlier battles and included many returned wounded. Their attitude was rather fatalistic than enthusiastic, while their discipline was extraordinarily high.

Each formation in turn had been rested in the back areas which lie between Amiens and Abbeville, and few will forget the peaceful charm of such villages as Picquigny, with its mediæval church and ruined castle perched upon a hill-top overlooking the village roofs and river.

At Picquigny, Edward IV of England and Louis XI held a Conference through a wooden trelliswork, " like that of a lion's cage," [1] on a bridge over the Somme. The village is much frequented by artists of the Corot school. It is most charming in autumn when the heavy foliage takes a golden and crimson colouring. And here at the entrance of the Rue des Chanoines a monument marks the spot where St. Firmin first preached Christianity. The Saint, known as St. Firmin the Martyr, was first Bishop of Amiens, and was beheaded by the Roman magistrate Sebastianus Xalerius. To the Saint and Martyr, the third bishop, St. Firmin the Confessor, erected the first Cathedral of Amiens.

While young soldiers swam and plunged in the river, Generals and more sophisticated men would steal away to some back reach and cast a fly upon the waters. There is a château in Condé-Folies from which the inhabitants had retired and whose roof was in a sad state of repair, with an immense cellerage, in whose pillared vaults more than one feast has been given. While up on the downs behind Picquigny stands the château of Cavillon, wherein dwelt the Comtesse de Haute Clocque, who, with dainty daughters, would appear as patron of Horse Shows, Race Meetings and other sporting events held by many Divisions upon the broad acres of the park. But Longpré, to whose railway station the British added many sidings, although a hospitable town, was possessed of the atmosphere of the condemned cell, for it was upon these sidings that trains were drawn up to remove the troops, concentrated from their billets, ready to carry them back to the smitten wastes of the battlefield.

[1] Comines.

The weather that had blazed with sun throughout July and early August had turned to pitiless rain. The roads, which at the best of times were ill-founded, had long since ceased to possess any stable foundation. Into the deep mud which formed their surface tree trunks and balks of timber were thrown to support the unceasing wheeled traffic. But, think with pity on the men who staggered and slithered, their feet often trapped between heavy sleepers, as the unseen road-bottom, on which they trod through twelve inches of slime, rocked and swayed beneath the weight of passing waggons.

The agonies of the battlefield were not alone due to the terrors of shell-fire and the lash of machine guns, nor even to the piteous wail of the wounded, but they were increased a hundredfold by the exertions required in going up to the line, and in retreating therefrom when relieved. Often would men have preferred to risk the peril of the front posts to the almost intolerable journeys back to comparative sanctuary. These roads, registered to an inch by the enemy artillery, were under incessant shell-fire, their scuppers and banks heaped with the corpses of mules and horses and with shattered waggons.

To retrieve the wounded from the festering quagmires into which had sunk the brick-dust of what once had been the villages of Guillemont and Guinchy, required four men, sometimes more, for each single stretcher ; while as they struggled beneath its weight they sank often knee-deep in mud. The vast cavities of shell-holes filled with oozing slime almost as soon as the fury of the exploding metal had expended itself; and into these death-traps drivers hastening with ammunition to the guns, or struggling forward with limbers, would plunge their animals, lost beyond hope of recovery. Looking at the new Guillemont and Guinchy, lying in the pleasant valley just west of the Flers Ridge, it is difficult now to believe that such horrors ever existed in their neighbourhood, still less that men could have endured them.

Although in Lord Haig's mind there was apparently no set objective to the First Battle of the Somme, it is apparent that optimism led him to expect objectives far beyond anything attained, and in fact with their horizon not limited by Thiepval, Bapaume and Péronne, or even by the prize of Cambrai and St. Quentin.

The Second Battle of the Somme, in March, 1918, was fought over the desolated fields marked by the earlier struggles. The bewildering and crushing events which commenced on 21st March, followed by swift recriminations and the immediate removal of Sir Hubert Gough, the Army Commander, have largely befogged what actually transpired when the whole of the ground captured in 1916 was retaken by the enemy, who pressed his victory through Albert and up to the very gates of Amiens.

The bitter controversy which arose has no place in this record. Yet simple facts serve to illumine the darkness of the tragedy that overtook the British Army holding the line upon which with such bloodshed the British posts in the west were sustained.

Let us look at those facts. On the 21st March, General von Hutier, with forty-six Divisions and over

5,000 guns, assailed the Fifth Army holding forty-one miles of front with fifteen Divisions. Over-whelmed from the first minute of the onslaught, hopelessly outnumbered, their trenches pulverized, their thin lines penetrated at every point, unsupported by any kind of reinforcements and beyond hope of aid, the unbroken line was driven back 5,000 yards. No more. And here it held.

The fate of isolated posts, of whole companies surrounded, but fighting to the last man, and of thousands of men, is wholly unknown. The fact remains that not more than 5,000 yards of a battle-field, on which scarcely one brick of a village stood upon another, and whereon every kind of vegetation had been blasted and withered, scorched and bleached until scarcely any green thing showed itself above the ground, was surrendered to the enemy.

It is not possible to analyse closely the German losses along the whole front; but in the monster battles of the Somme, on the Lys and before Kemmel, on the British front alone the enemy lost 3,860 officers killed, among 16,000 casualties, and 419,000 among the rank and file. Nor did the Second Battle of the Somme succeed in destroying the morale of the British Army. Though forced to surrender valuable ground, to leave behind prisoners, guns, war material and not least their cemeteries, and to witness the battle-line everywhere receding, the morale of the Army was not even weakened. In a war of attrition the Second Battle of the Somme may be regarded not as a British defeat, for upon those blood-soaked fields, as on those of the Valley of the Lys, German hopes were shattered, and the ambitions of Ludendorff found their nemesis.

On the other side of the picture, it seems almost unbelievable that the German Armies, after suffering years of attrition, hedged in by blockade, surrounded by enemies, could have thrown themselves with such impetus again into the fight. They stormed the stoutest defences. They hurled themselves against lines, so often fashioned by themselves, whose almost impregnable strength they had tested in defence. No matter how great their losses they charged towards the victory which seemed within their grasp.

The Second Battle of the Somme seems even more hideous than the first. Not one village, or copse, or post, which witnessed the furies of the fighting in 1916, was saved from its further bath of blood. But there are few who can tell the detailed story of all that occurred. The perfected war machine was fully possessed of its gifts of horror. The first bombardment was accompanied by gas— phosgene, mustard gas, and the terrible " Blue Cross," invisible gas. For more than eight hours on end the defenders, for not one second, could discard their masks. Dazed and sorely tried, officers in charge of staggering, semi-conscious men moved through the mists of gas to which Nature had added her powerful screen, attempting to link a line which meant so much on the map, but, on the ground, little more than stunted trees and unending wastes of shell-holes. And the attack with its single objective, the West, swept over the opposition, surrounded it and struck it to the ground wherever it was met. The Fifth Army has no need of an apologia, for it played a notable part in the coming victory.

The Somme battlefield is a prelude to the victories in the east, for again, across the scarred ridge, " the Flers Line," a war-worn sword with blood on it, rising across the centre of the field, there was played out the first act of the last great drama whose curtain was the Armistice of November 11th.

Already early in July, 1918, the great counter-attack under the supreme command of Marshal Foch had commenced south of the Somme. A brilliant action, engaging especially Canadians and Australians, was fought between the Somme and the Avre, with its centre on the railway running east–west between the rivers. Infantry accompanied by Tanks carried the line back approximately to our former front line of the 1st July, 1916. The rolling downs by Chipilly and Morlancourt were scenes of furious fighting; and in this Americans took their place, shoulder to shoulder with the British. The attack of August the 8th before Amiens marked the turning of the tide; and therefrom there followed tremendous events, an historic procession, wherein all the battlefields of Picardy were again battlefields; and, in the after stages, vast areas of military organization.

How chilling were the scenes even to those who poured through to victory and pursuit, scapes whose skies were always so Corotesque, but whose ground was an inferno studded with bleaching wooden crosses!

The traveller must be in a hurry if he would keep pace with the advance to the great Hindenburg Line, for with great bounds, Division leaping over Division, it swept on to the east. Between the 21st and 31st August the Third and Fourth Armies, Byng and Rawlinson, had recaptured the whole of the Somme battlefield, and had moved ten miles to the east of the Flers Ridge. Péronne had fallen: Bapaume had heard the blare of British bands. But the Germans entrenched themselves in front of Cambrai and the Canal de St. Quentin, their defences focused at Epéhy, where was marshalled the redoubtable Alpine Corps from Bavaria, still fresh, despite its wounds at Kemmel, from unbroken victory in the east. Epéhy, Gouzeaucourt, Villers Guislain, Queant on the fringe of the Arras battle-field, mark the course of the Hindenburg Line, the last entrenched German stronghold east of the Rhine.

There was here fought by the Germans the greatest rearguard action of all history. The hour of victory had passed. Only defence to the death could minimize the greater punishment of humiliating defeat. In these last entrenchments the Germans offered a resistance of unqualified strength and gallantry. Machine gunners died at their posts. Time after time the shattered Battalions of Germans hurled themselves in counter-attack against those to whom Foch cried " *Marchez aux canons !* " and who, undismayed by losses, followed victory to the very mouths of the guns.

The front of these Titanic battles covered twenty-five miles of country, north and south. The road through Bapaume, Marcoing, Solesmes, Le Quesnoy, Maubeuge, marked the centre of the battlefields.

These are divided into eight areas, marking distinct phases of the advance and of the resistance. There was the attack of the Fourth Army between the 8th and 12th August in the Battle of Amiens, followed by the Battle of Bapaume between the 21st and 31st August, in which the Third and Fourth Armies took part, capturing 34,250 prisoners and 270 guns ; while in the same period the First Army fought the Second Battle of Arras on the left flank.

There followed a lull in the easterly drive in front of the defences of the Hindenburg Line. Throughout September, the Third and Fourth Armies, incurring immense losses, fought for mastery of the ridge which lies to the immediate west of the St. Quentin canal. It was here, in the Battle of Epéhy, that the German Alpine Corps, and the famous Bavarian Leib Regiment,[1] made their last stand in the west. The villages of Gouzeaucourt, Hermies, Heudicourt, Epéhy, Hargicourt were scenes of the bitterest fighting. No matter that the political structure behind the German Armies on the Western Front was crumbling with disillusion and the civil population seething with revolution, that the armies were on short rations, the Germans fought with unsurpassed gallantry at every point. To British heroism there are memorials in this area to the 42nd Division, to the Royal Newfoundlanders, to the 12th Division and to the Loyal North Lancashire Regiment.

[1] Comradeship, the legacy of war, with the years grows in strength. I record with pride that having fought against the K.B. Inf.-Leib-Regiment at Bailleul and Epéhy, and having been received by its members in 1933, '34, '35, I was elected to *Ehrenmitglied* (honorary membership) of the Leib regiments—Kameradschaft.

The Hindenburg Line cracked, and then was broken. September 29th is the date upon which the British Armies began their great drive to the east, scarcely interrupted, despite the opposition— an advance planned by Haig himself, whose speed and élan astonished the world and not least the Generalissimo, Marshal Foch. With rare generosity, the Generalissimo came personally to Sir Douglas Haig to congratulate him upon the success of the British Armies.

The attack of the 29th was preceded by an event of peculiar interest. The Canal de St. Quentin disappears underground at the village of Vendhuille, and for a distance of 6,000 yards running south it forms a subterranean gallery, 50 feet below the ground surface and 70 feet wide. This tunnel dated from the First Empire and upon its arches bore the " N " of the first Napoleon. German ingenuity had converted this tunnel into a military work of extraordinary strength, with numerous bolt-holes, leading forwards and backwards, their mouths, concreted, being machine-gun fortresses. The waterway was occupied by barges into which a whole Division could be placed wholly immune from the heaviest bombardment. And immediately to the west lay the strongest part of the Hindenburg Line.

Before the general advance could begin, it was imperative to stifle such a hornet's nest; and this difficult task was entrusted to the Australians and the new American Divisions, the " Tar Heels," which had been trained under British tutelage south of Ypres, in front of Zillebeke. Men from the city of

New York, from the cotton and tobacco fields of Carolina, and from the rugged mountains of Tennessee, advanced shoulder to shoulder with those from Australia and Britain. The detailed story of the routing out of the enemy from this labyrinth with gas and bombs remains wherever the English language is spoken. But the success of the enterprise was the necessary overture to the general advance of the First, Third and Fourth Armies on a twenty-five mile front in the Cambrai–St. Quentin Battle, which on the 29th and 30th September leaped ten miles forward with a capture of 36,500 prisoners and 580 guns.

Nor was this great advance easy, for the Germans held tenaciously, their rear guards and isolated machine-gun posts perishing almost to a man. There is a cluster of five cemeteries between Villers Guislain and Vendhuille, villages which marked the fearful execution of the Battalions which opened the attack. In the Targelle Ravine, and half a mile south in Pigeon Ravine, platoon after platoon was wrecked by machine-gun fire and fell, their faces to the enemy, young officers at their head. Rows and rows of men, from Worcestershire and Surrey and from Scotland, lay stretched on the grass in these quiet valleys; while on the highest point between the valleys, at Meath Post, the dead lay thick around a strong point now marked by a Cemetery.

But the 29th September witnessed the first real break in the stubborn resistance. Across the bodies of their fallen comrades the advance swept on, smothering resistance wherever it was found. Beyond the Canal lay the open country, and within view from Meath Post were villages untouched by shell-fire, church spires, crops and woods, gold and russet, hung with autumn foliage. Troops, wearied beyond belief, yet stormed on, with the vision of the break-through, even of Berlin. No leash would hold them : they experienced the sense, tingling and triumphant, of victory. And as they entered such villages as Clary, Villers-Outreaux and the outskirts of Cambrai, hardy peasants who had withstood the bitterness of four years of invasion acclaimed the victors almost as the enemy departed from their gates.

In Clary, by some miracle, French flags were produced and a gramophone wheezed " La Marseillaise " as Scottish troops marched in. King George V visited Clary shortly after the Armistice, and those who had captured the village, the 5th Scottish Rifles, formed the Guard of Honour. The square in front of the *Mairie* was renamed the " *Place des Écossais*."

The advance was moving towards the historic battlefield of Malplaquet ; and it is interesting to note that, after this bloody affray in 1709, Cambrai was crowded with fugitives, to whom the immortal Fénelon, commonly called the " Swan of Cambrai," [1] threw open his Palace to receive them. Every corner of the Palace was occupied, corridors, staircases, rooms great and small. A hundred and fifty officers, whether French or prisoners of war, the Archbishop received at once at his table. " God will help us," he said. " Providence has infinite

[1] *Galignani's Guide through France.*

THE HARVEST OF BATTLE

C. R. W. Nevinson.

THE OUTSKIRTS OF LENS

Ian Strang.

resources on which I confidently rely. Only let us give all we have : it is my duty and my pleasure." [1] Besides the Palace and monument erected " to the memory of this virtuous ecclesiastical dignitary," the British victors and German prisoners of war received the merciful aid of the Red Cross.

In the battles which followed during October, there is much which recalls the situation which faced Marlborough in 1709. Just as Crécy and Azincourt recall the traditional characteristics of British warriors, unchanged through the centuries, so the new battles of Cambrai–St. Quentin reproduced that of Malplaquet, focused on the same ground. " Starving as were the French soldiers, they flung away their rations in the eagerness for the fight, and fell back at its close in serried masses, which no efforts of Marlborough could break. They had lost 12,000 men, but the forcing their lines of entrenchments had caused the Allies a loss of double that number." [2] So writes Green, the English historian. France was exhausted, as was Germany. The terrible slaughter which bears the name of the Battle of Malplaquet testifies equally to the fighting qualities of the German rear-guards in the country-side west of the Forêt de Mormal, on whose out-skirts Malplaquet lies. History was repeated. The Allied losses between the end of July and the Armistice exceeded those of Germany by nearly 150,000 men, not double, as in Marlborough's battles, but a figure greatly in excess of the defence. The vigour and audacity of Marlborough's plans astonished

[1] *Fénelon à Cambrai*, par Emmanuel de Broglie.
[2] *A Short History of the English People*, by Green. Vol. II.

I

the cautious strategists of his day, as those of Haig
surprised Marshal Foch.[1]

Winston Churchill, the very Gibbon and Macaulay
of twentieth-century English History, refers to the
generosity of Marlborough " amongst the wounded
officers of the enemy after the Battle of Malplaquet." [2] Haig's officers were no less magnanimous.
A Battalion Commander, writing afterwards, records :

> British and Germans were treated alike ; and beside
> me lay a young Bavarian, his chin still hairless, one of the
> Alpine Corps, from mountains I knew and loved, with a
> shattered thigh and other grievous injuries. His face was
> pale and the eyes very bright. Orderlies and nurses
> looked at him every now and again to see how he fared.
> And while others groaned, and some shrieked with agony,
> he never uttered a sound. Only when night fell and the
> lamps were lighted did he begin to whimper quietly. His
> hand lay stretched out hanging over the coverlet. I
> sometimes glanced at the lad. He was crying like a child,
> so I touched his hand, and he held on. I think that made
> his passage easier, for he sighed and smiled at me and a
> little later he slept. Then they took the body away.[3]

The immensity of the War machine may have
engulfed men in its octopus embrace, but it did
not destroy the chivalry which had characterized the
marches of Marlborough no less than those of King
Harry.

Between the 8th and 10th October, Cambrai fell,
and the Armies mopped up a host of villages on a
front of fifteen miles and to a depth of twelve. To
the east, Solesmes and Le Cateau now marked the

[1] Compare *The World Crisis*, by Winston Churchill. Critique
of Foch and Haig, pp. 801 to 805.

[2] *Marlborough, his Life and Times*, by Winston Churchill, p. 475.

[3] *Warrior*, by Lt.-Col. G. S. Hutchison.

frontier, while a further 12,000 prisoners and 250 guns were left behind.

The whole countryside is dotted with cemeteries. There are more than fifty between Cambrai and Le Cateau, farther separated from one another than those of the Somme, and marking phases of the War vastly different in technique. The veterans of 1914 lie beside the younger brothers who crowned victory with their blood. At Le Cateau is the Memorial to the 19th Infantry Brigade, the same whose Highland officers, claymore in hand, as did the clansmen of all history, advanced to meet the grey hordes of the enemy; and the young men, repeating history, armed with grenades, stormed again across the graves in which slept Scotsmen, Welsh and Cockneys. No Brigade in the Army throughout the war years had been subjected to more severe tests in battle after battle. Ploeg-steert, Loos, High Wood and Les Bœufs were already dimming memories. Arras and the Lys were almost forgotten. But the return to Le Cateau! The stand before Le Cateau in 1914, where the Thin Red Line reincarnated its Crimean glory, contributed to this Brigade an imperishable halo.

Strange things happen in war. It was from a wardrobe in the village of Clary that a British trooper emerged after four years' imprisonment therein. As a prisoner he had been kept from capture by the enemy by the singular devotion of a peasant woman, who, although German soldiers were billeted in her house, sleeping but a few feet from where the English trooper was hidden, kept

him alive and well until the British advance freed
him to return to the ranks of his own Regiment
and join in the pursuit of the invaders. There is
no stranger tale from these battlefields, and none
which better illustrates the tenacity of the peasant
or the fortitude and patience of the British private
soldier.

Again the great battle surges forward, the First
and Third and Fourth Armies co-operating in
another great blow against the struggling lines of
the enemy. The 17th to the 25th October witnessed a further penetration of five miles to the east
on a front of twenty miles between Valenciennes
and the village of Andigny south of Le Cateau.
Officially, this battle is known as that of the " Selle
River," and the passage of the river in the face of
tremendous opposition was a feat of great daring
and of high military skill.

> British sappers submerged waist-high in the chilling
> currents, motionless under a hail of bullets which threshed
> the stream, bore on their shoulders strips of plank over
> which passed the Infantry of the Line. The engineers
> of one Division, under cover of darkness on the 11th
> October, constructed eleven foot-bridges before dawn
> from pontoons driven to the river bed.[1]

The British Armies in the Battle of the Selle
reached Valenciennes with their left wing. They
were held before Le Quesnoy and Landrecies ;
and in the further drive to the east were faced with
the formidable obstacles of the vast Forêt de Mormal
and the Sambre River. The forest is twelve miles
deep and some seven miles across. No one knew

[1] *33rd Division in France and Flanders*, p. 141.

to what extent in its darkened recesses the enemy might be hiding, or if he was prepared to offer a resistance which would recall, even on a grimmer scale, the untold secret horrors of High Wood. There had been desperate fighting in the little village of Englefontaine, where no sign of the coming collapse of the German resistance was exhibited. On the outskirts of the Forest, the bayonet, which for so long in trench warfare had been relegated to the homely duties of a toasting-fork, again became the *arme blanche*. There were tremendous hand-to-hand encounters between grenadiers on the fringe of the trees ; while in the undergrowth silent duels were fought out between bayonet-fighters and snipers.

Some evidence of the relief of the inhabitants in this zone, so close during the four years to the gargantuan struggles on the Somme, is provided by the simple message recorded hereunder.

To G.O.C., 33rd Division.

The Mairie of Englefontaine, which met this afternoon in a cellar of this village, begs to express to you in the name of the 1,200 inhabitants freed by the British Army its deepest feeling of heartfelt gratitude.

From O.C., French Mission, 33rd Division.[1]

Graceful as is all this countryside of Picardy in the spring of lilacs and apple blossom, in the summer of yellowing corn and bright green trees and root crops, in the autumn when the heavy foliage takes a golden and crimson colouring and the plough has turned again the dark red loam,

---

[1] *33rd Division in France and Flanders*, p. 149.

it is in winter that the battlefields recapture something of the bleakness which the metal hurricane of war produced. The ice-laden winds which sweep across the dominating plateaux, search the valleys and whistle through the naked branches of the woods, are those which lashed the warrior in his trenches and smote him with their fierce blasts as, living in the open fields, without any kind of shelter, equipped lightly for the onward rush and coming victory, he marches towards Maubeuge.

The Allied Drive is incomparable in all the annals of military history. No Huns of Attila charged more eagerly to the attack. No Paladins of Charlemagne more proudly carried the course of victory on their pennants. The troops of Marlborough at Malplaquet never harried the enemy more fiercely. Those of Napoleon at Austerlitz never more gloriously swept the enemy from the field; nor when the French armies, conquering the Alpine peaks, charged down upon the bounteous plains of Piedmont were they more zealous in their quest for conquest. Not those of Wellington at Waterloo. Not Jackson at Gettysburg, nor Von Moltke at Gravelotte. Not when the Prussian overthrew the Third Napoleon and destroyed his armies before Paris. Not the armies of Kitchener who sent the Khalifa's hordes flying from the battlefield of Omdurman. Nor yet the soldiers of Marshal Oku when the Russians fled from Port Arthur. No warriors in all history so applied themselves to the business of victory.

And on the German side, while Hindenburg and Ludendorff, the Kaiser and his statesmen put their heads together seeking for a formula which might save their Armies and the German nation from defeat and ruin, no warriors in all history, be it said, in the hour of their defeat, fought with greater courage and skill than the German Armies thrown from the impregnable defences of the Hindenburg Line.[1]

---

[1] *Warrior.*

The Great War, indeed all modern warfare, provides little opportunity for the chivalries which were both the prelude to action and so often that which characterized the battlefields of modern history. The Great War was the killing of the unseen by the unknown; but when the opposing sides came into close contact with one another as they did on the Somme, except in the close fighting with bomb and bayonet, " an eye for an eye and a tooth for a tooth," there were during moments of respite from action many instances of kindly humanity, both recorded and untold, on both sides, which demonstrate that even in the bitterest of battles the soldier serves no personal animosity.

Over the whole of the British front on the Somme, the detailed history of the War records gallantry in the face of fearful odds, unmarked in any other era of human history. The Somme was the first great test of strength between the British and German Armies. The British Army was a force incomparable in morale and equipment, gathered for the attack, while that in defence was steeped in the military traditions of the world's mightiest military power. If British soldiers stormed and stormed again, across the dead bodies of their companions, hosts which were impregnable, the German defence, so frequently surrounded, with war-worn guns and short of rations, fought back with no less tenacity and valour.

CHAPTER VI

LAST PHASE OF THE ATTACK—SELLE AND
SAMBRE

Forêt de Mormal—Eye-witness account of the crossing of the Sambre River—Supplies outrun—Victory.

WE enter now upon the last phase of the War, the final battle, fought no less fiercely than any of its predecessors, known as that of Valenciennes–Maubeuge–Mons, between the 1st and 11th November.

The passage of the Forest was accomplished without much difficulty until the villages of Sart Bara and Berlaimont were reached. But the River Sambre presented enormous difficulties. The German Army had strongly entrenched itself on the high ground south of Maubeuge, commanding the river. The tale of its passage glows with heroism, and is typical of the kind of fighting undertaken and inspired by the British Army in these later battles. Here is the story, an eye-witness account, of the crossing of the river at one point.

.   .   .   .   .

A breathless hush, one which could be felt. The crash of shells and crack of bullets seemed remote. A bit jingled : the strain on leather traces could be heard as the animals were wheeled into position.

The ground between the house, behind which cover was taken, and the river bank consisted of low shrubs and a few trees, dotted here and there. A broad pathway through a garden led from one side. The drivers gathered their reins and turned their horses' heads, two on each side, ready for the order to go forward. The shrill staccato of machine guns and the loud crack of bursting shrapnel deafened the ears.

" Are you ready ? " cried the Transport Officer above the din.

Assent was dimly heard as the men crouched over the necks of their animals.

" Go ! " shouted the Transport Officer.

Spurs bit deep into the flesh of the straining animals, whips descended with a thwack upon their flanks. They leaped forward, turning from the cover of the building into the open.

Twenty yards. The mules had gathered speed. Thirty, forty yards. Almost half-way, the limbers rolling and crashing through the undergrowth, drivers' whips goading the animals forward. The onlookers, recklessly exposing themselves from cover, cheered and yelled with excitement. Fifty yards. The driver on the right flank fell limp in his saddle : the near-side animal plunged, stumbled and fell headlong with its rider, dragging the off-side animal down. Men from cover rushed forward to the driver's aid.

Sixty yards, more than half-way. The trio, resembling the chariot race of a Roman arena, crashed forward, leaving the fallen amid carnage kicking hideously in the tangled traces. Another storm of bullets struck the riders. A second driver, throwing his hands upwards, his head and chest torn by bullets, toppled backwards on to the pole between his wounded animals. Slightly ahead, they swerved across a third limber, fouling its wheels. Seventy

yards. Eighty yards. The waggon tilted danger-
ously, one wheel spinning in the air. The driver
laid his mules over, steadying the bounding limber.
Another crash of bullets, and the mules in the right
flank limber fell headlong, throwing the waggon on
to its side, the driver falling, being pinned under a
wheel. Ten yards, the curling river beneath the
eyes, an eight-foot plunge to death or sanctuary.

One driver alone had stayed the course. Blooded
spurs bit deep. Again the whip descended, while
reins were gathered tightly to keep the mules' heads
straight to the water. Under the savage spike of
spurs and lash of whip, the mules leaped from the
river bank far into the stream. The spinning
wheels came after. The flat bottom of the limber
met the water with a smack. A great splash
went up.

One driver had reached his goal. The limber
wheels settled on the bottom of the river. The
driver held the mules' heads against the current.
Snorting with terror they strove to reach the farther
bank, dragging the limber, as the driver steered it
across the river. Holding tightly to the reins, the
man drew out a jack-knife and opened its blade
with his teeth, then slipped from the saddle and
cut the traces. The mules surged forward, free.
They turned to the current and were carried down-
stream, the driver seizing hold of the limber and
crawling to security. He was under cover, squatting
in about eighteen inches of water while bullets
hailed overhead. He could not get back to the
bank. He must await events.

Sharp eyes watching the enemy entrenchments had spotted the machine gun in particular which had occasioned the worst damage. Already volunteers had stripped themselves to go forward, carrying ropes and balks of timber to lash to the limbers if the venture had proved successful. Some had crept forward to give succour to the casualties. Men, bootless and stripped to the waist, had volunteered to build the bridge. Four more limbers stood ready under cover to run the gauntlet of fire. From a corner of the building, the Colonel surveyed the enemy position through his field glasses.

" It looks as if we've got the worst machine gun under control now," he muttered to the Transport Officer by his side. " We've got one limber to the river bottom, but it needs three at least to carry these timbers. I expect we can haul them into position once we get them into the river bed. We'll have another shot at it, if your men are ready."

". . . almost suicide," he muttered to himself . . . " men have got the V.C. cheaper than this . . . much cheaper." He glanced at the drivers and noted them. The Corporal, a North-country yeoman, a veteran from South Africa, and a mere boy. Almost involuntarily the Colonel ejaculated : " What are you doing there, lad ? . . . You're a wounded man."

" My mules, sir. My job," replied the lad, a challenge in his eyes, a smile quivering on his lips.

The Colonel's heart groaned. . . . Eighteen. . . .

But the lad sat smiling, facing immediate, almost certain death. And there was the fourth driver, old soldier, begrimed South African ribbons on his tunic, old enough to be the father, almost the grandfather, of the lad at his side. Someone was whistling between his teeth: "Oh, it's a lovely war!" Whistling and singing as men will to stifle the fear and horror in their hearts.

"Are you ready?" cried the Colonel. "As soon as the limbers have gone, you other lads begin to get forward with the timber. Swimmers with ropes first. For God's sake keep low and take all the cover you can. Spread well out and make for the river anywhere. Once you're in the water, you're under cover. Remember that. . . . Right! All ready with the limbers? Good luck and go like hell!"

The men gathered their reins.

"Go!" cried the Transport Officer.

For one brief second the Colonel closed his eyes, a prayer to the God Unknown of the battlefield frozen on his lips.

Again from the cover of the building there debouched four men, four animals and four limbers, racing for the river edge. The enemy from his point of vantage was waiting in expectation for further movement from this quarter. White puffs of shrapnel, accompanied by a loud crack and the tearing of tree trunks and branches, followed the appearance of the cavalcade. A machine gun traversed the front. The animals plunged forward. The Colonel's eyes were upon the bent backs, fear in his heart. . . . These men played a part in the pageant of heroism and of terror. Danger, deadly danger was present, dogging the footsteps and ahead. On either side death lurked tugging at the reins, luring the unwary to the wreckage from which waved arms and legs, beckoning. And death shrieked suddenly from on high, breathing fire and gas and molten metal, and roaring his laughter in great gusts as man rode and ducked and swayed and bobbed, stifling laughter, mocking the vale of tears.

Immediately in the wake of the limber, half-naked figures, usually in pairs, began to worm their way forwards, carrying timber balks and doors. Others, by swifter rushes, carried ropes. The enemy's fire was wilder, less concentrated, under the punishment of the thirty-two machine guns hammering their lines. Here was stupendous spectacle, accompanied throughout by giant symphony of sound. The thunderous roar of the guns exceeded pandemonium. The chatter of machine guns throbbed maniac melody to the peal of cannon. It was as if giants beat a thousand tom-toms, while raving fanatics smote all the instruments of death, in wild disharmony. One sound alone for each man beat with deafening certainty, a heart knocking in a wheezing throat.

Almost so soon as the limbers turned into the open, a burst of fire smote the waggon driven by the Corporal. The man uttered a stifled cry and slid from the saddle, his face and shoulders flecked with blood. The wood-work of the limber ripped and tore, a wheel splintered. The maddened, wounded mules swerved and turned, presenting a broadside target to the enemy. A second later another burst of fire bit deeply into their flesh and they collapsed in the wreckage. The other three waggons crashed forwards unscathed.

On the left, the yeoman with a pair of blacks, his head lying between their necks, shouted encouragement and threats, spurring and striking as he forced their sleek bodies forward. His was a clear course down the garden path, and he forged ahead. In the centre, the veteran, uttering strange oaths, reviled his chestnuts as they strained at the traces. A gap appeared where the corporal and his team had been cut short in their journey; and on the right, the lad, astride a light-footed dun, whispered an urgent message in the ear of the offside animal. Bullets cracked the air like a whiplash, but on sped the limbers. Seventy yards and the veteran crashed, his steel helmet battered through the brain, the chestnuts a squealing, bullet-ridden mass of kicking horseflesh. But the fire was less severe, less well directed, though every second and every yard was filled with imminent danger.

The first successful driver, astride the limber in mid-stream, had heard the thunder of the hoofs, and glancing anxiously towards the brink of the near bank, suddenly saw the terrified eyes and leaping legs of two mules above him, and then the tense face of the yeoman beneath its steel helmet. As the first mules leaped, their heads held short and high by their driver's strong arm, the familiar dun heads of the lad's pair came to view. The air above him cracked, and within a split second the clear picture of a boy and the animal's heads was diffused in a cascade of blood. The yeoman's team plunged, the limber anchoring in the river bottom. The other team, smitten as they sprang, tumbled headlong into the water, dragging the limber after them. Eddies of red blood mingled themselves with the curling waters. The waiting driver, appalled by horror for one brief moment, plunged into the stream and grabbed the lad by the arm. His hand snatched the submerged traces fixed to the limber, and, clinging desperately against the force of the current, he struggled for position and to bring the stricken man to his side. He dragged the lad on to the limber where a moment earlier he himself had been standing.

" 'Ullo, ole soaker; where do I put this 'ere limber?" called the yeoman to the driver, as he eased his spluttering mules. " I'd make me fortune at the 'Ippodrome! . . . but I wouldn't do it again fer ten thasand quid."

How casual, how matter-of-fact it sounded! Nothing cynical in those words, simply cheerful comradeship, even where death claimed two or more from every four.

The driver glanced round, holding the lad above the swirling waters.

" Better pull over as close to the far bank as you can, in line with mine. Then cut the traces and let the mules go."

" Let 'em go? I'll swim 'em dahn-stream. It's

the first barf I've 'ad fer weeks. 'Specks I can land 'em lower dahn or find a foot'old until th' strafe's over."

The driver bent to the wounded man. Bullets had pierced the lung and shattered one shoulder. He breathed uneasily, and his lips were flecked with blood.

Snorting and protesting, the mules manœuvred the limber into position, and then, cutting the traces, the yeoman gathered his team and turned down-stream. Those remaining had but a moment to wait, for within seconds, men, the advance guard, began to slip one by one over the river bank down into the water; and within a few minutes others followed with the timber. Their faces and bodies were scratched from the undergrowth, but as they tumbled into the comparative haven of the river, they cried out with exaltation. First the lad's limber was dragged into position. Then timbers were lashed between the waggons, forming a foot-way from bank to bank. Very soon, with the help of doors, a roadway some four feet wide had been constructed about twelve inches below the surface of the water. Ropes were knotted and fastened from one bank to the other to provide a hand-rail. A bridge had been built.

While the improvisation was yet building, the Colonel had crept forward, elbowing his way to the river bank. His excitement was intense. The plan had been successful. Three limbers had been plunged into the river, and all around him through the undergrowth timbers were being carried forward to complete a bridge. The advance would not be held up. But many more lives would be lost if the enemy's machine-gun fire could not be subdued. Cries from the forest edge told of men being hit, and all around the Colonel as he crept forward the undergrowth was lashed and bitten by bullets.

Yet the Battalion was moving forward. Soon machine guns and riflemen would be able to achieve the passage, and then they would force the enemy from his position on the rising ground. The Colonel slipped under cover, over the river bank. Death from on high crackled his shrill staccato, but he could not touch the machine-gun commander now. Men, swimming and waist-high in water, were gathering the timbers and lashing them into position. As one after another slipped over the river edge, he clung to tufts of grass and roots, pulling himself along the bank to the head of the footbridge. Water above his knees, the Colonel reached the bridge. Among the first to come forward had been two signallers with their field telephone, trailing the line behind them; and they hacked a cavity in the farther bank, wherein they established an advance station.

" Are you connected ? " called the Colonel.

" All correct, sir," came the reply.

" I'll come over." The Colonel moved carefully on his injured leg over the now completed footway, while willing hands assisted his passage.

" Tell the O.C. A Company to speak. . . . That you ? Right ! . . . We've got the bridge across. Come forward as soon as you can. Send a message to the Worcesters and Queen's and back to the

K

nearest Brigade. I'll hoist a timber at the bridge-head so that you can mark it, but don't let the men bunch. I don't want the fire concentrated here. Get the men spread out along the river bank : they can make their way on the water edge to the bridge. The guns must go the nearest way, straight for the bridge-head, and chance it. But don't let the men bunch." He handed the receiver to the signaller ; and then, freed from the immediate action of the moment, turned to survey the scene and reflect. The bridge was completed. Each new piece of timber which came strengthened and widened the work. Those who had first arrived, their skins wet and glistening in the feeble November sun, stood shivering beside him under the farther bank. The water, lapping and gurgling against the timbers, rushed away, streaked with blood.

Within a few minutes, crawling men, dragging machine guns and ammunition boxes, began to slip over the edge of the river bank, and splashed through the water across the timbers. To the left were shrubs, and a little farther out a hedgerow meeting at a beet-sugar factory with its variety of outbuildings. The first four gun teams were ordered forward, taking cover behind shrubs and buildings, to move as best they could in order to outflank the enemy's position. The hostile machine-gun fire was heavy but intermittent, and against it there poured con-tinuously a stream of machine-gun fire, now well under control from the near bank. The Colonel turned to the telephone as a signaller handed the receiver to him.

" Sappers are going to make another bridge higher up," he muttered. " And the Queen's are heading for this bridge. . . . I hope they won't bunch."

He dug his heels into the mud and lay back against the river bank, awaiting events. There suddenly appeared the first riflemen of the Queen's, running breathlessly and splashing into the water at the bridge head. Five men, then two more; some dropped over the banks on either side of the bridge and came towards it. Three more, and then larger groups.

" Don't bunch ! " cried the Colonel, but it was too late. A German machine gun tore the ranks as a group hesitated for a fatal second. Faces and chests were torn as with a swift-moving saw. The men's bodies crumpled like sacks and pitched headlong into the river. The men had been extended in their approach to the river, but as they came nearer they began to edge towards the raised timber marking the bridge-head. It seemed so short a run, the risk so small, thus to find quickly cover from the hail of shrapnel and machine-gun bullets which bit their extended ranks. A group on the right rose and ran for the bridge-head. Simultaneously, another in the centre surged towards it. A German machine gun, finding new position, and momentarily free from the hail of lead, opened fire. As had happened a moment earlier, another group of Surrey riflemen was hewn and overwhelmed by the storm of steel. Some toppled into the water, others fell on the bank, while others turned to fly. They met another group, and still more men running towards the bridge-head. Into the struggling mass poured machine-gun fire. Killed and wounded fell into the water, some being carried down the stream, others being locked against the limber wheels. The Colonel watched aghast. More and more men, mostly mere lads, reinforcements, came into his line of vision, steel-helmeted heads and tunicked torsos. Then a murderous burst of fire tore their ranks, and they pitched and rolled into the bloody waters. Some few, clinging to their arms, were astride the bridge, terror-stricken but unharmed, a young subaltern among them.

" Take what men you've got," said the Colonel grimly, " and get forward. Knock that machine gun out of action or there'll be more murder."

The lad, seated in a limber, swirling red waters around him, appeared dazed.

" Look sharp ! " ordered the Colonel. The voice of authority wiped out the sheer horror of a lost platoon.

The Colonel gripped the telephone and spoke.

" For God's sake tell the Queen's not to bunch. Each man must make his own way to the river. It's safe, safe, don't you understand, under the river bank. But it's bloody murder if they bunch."

Even as he spoke a howitzer opened fire. The turmoil heightened in its fury. The ground heaved and shuddered : great tufts of earth were hurled through the air. The descending metal bore down upon the dead and the wounded, grinding battered bodies to pulp, or throwing dismembered limbs high into the air. Oncoming men reeled and staggered in the carnage, while others, cursing the universe, leaped and scrambled over the mounting parapet of dead and dying in an endeavour to reach the bridge-head.

And more and more men stumbled against the growing heap of dead and wounded above the bank, and they were smitten, crashing headlong, if not already dead, to a fate by drowning. Within a minute or two, more than eighty men had perished at the bridge-head. Twenty-three alone had survived ; and still they came in fearful, horrified groups, five or ten yards alone between absolute safety and certain death. The crack and thud of a stream of bullets met each group as it surged into the trap, hammering faces and bodies into pulp. But all the time single riflemen and machine gunners, creeping through the scrub, and crawling over the river bank, escaped the concentrated fire and crossed the bridge to the other side. At immense cost, the opposition to the enemy was being erected, the firing line being built. The battle was going forwards.

By nightfall the enemy had been thrust from the ridge, and with the exception of intermittent shelling, including salvoes of gas shells, the following night was quiet. From the right, it was learned that Le Cateau had been recaptured. The British Army was back upon the historic battle-ground of Mons, where in August, more than four years earlier, the first few Divisions had withstood the massed onslaught of the most powerful army in the world. November 7th, 1918. Troops well-nigh exhausted must continue the pursuit. During the fighting some Battalions had been reduced to half their strength. The river banks were thick with dead, the waters swollen with blood. Men tightened their belts and went on : the road to Maubeuge ; some said, to Berlin. But how to go farther without food and ammunition, except that the enemy seemed to have faded from the landscape over-night ? To go on. . . . Whither ? How ? Who knew ? Advance. . . .

It must be remembered that the advancing armies had far outstripped their supplies. The roads had been heavily mined by the retreating enemy and were constantly disrupted by delayed explosions. The railways had been torn up and bridges destroyed. The narrow roads seethed with endless columns of forward-moving transport, troops, ammunition and supplies, and were thick with ambulances, walking wounded and thousands of prisoners of war.

The forward line fought almost without rations, while those coming to their aid had for the most part distributed what they carried among the civilian population in the relieved villages through which they marched. And here was presented a further problem to the advancing army. A considerable population was left behind, which must be fed ; while tens of thousands of prisoners, marching west, across the naked Somme battlefields, exhausted to the limit of human endurance, were almost sixty miles from the nearest railhead.

No one who witnessed the grey ranks of Germany

in grey November, as they straggled to the west, could regard German soldiers in defeat without pity. Did not " *Liebe Heimat* " mean as much to the German as " Home, Sweet Home " to Englishmen, or the bosom of his family to the French *poilu* ?

Many of the British soldiers went hungry and within a few hours fought on an empty stomach that some mud-grimed unshaven soldier of the enemy should receive sustenance ; while many others emptied their haversacks that village children should not starve. At Sart Bara the inhabitants delivered an eloquent message, which in its original form is worthy of reproduction.

Commandant la 33rd Division.

À Monsieur le Général,

MONSIEUR LE GÉNÉRAL,

Permettez à une population éprouvée par le joug le plus odieux que l'histoire ait connu de venir déposer à vos pieds l'expression de sa reconnaissance la plus sincère et de son dévouement le plus absolu. Pendant plus de quatre ans, nous avons gémi sous la botte teutonne, nous avons connu toutes les humiliations, toutes les injustices, toutes les violences.

Nous avons vu élever à la hauteur d'une institution nationale le vol, le délation, la courtisanerie. Et nos cœurs et nos ames se sont répliés comme des fleurs trop délicates sous un souffle glacé.

Mais un jour s'est levé, Monsieur le Général, ou grâce à votre science militaire, grâce à l'incomparable valeur de l'armée Britannique, nos malheurs se sont évanouis comme au soleil-levant s'envolent les fantômes de la nuit.

Monsieur le Général, nous vous disons le merci le plus profond que nos cœurs puissent ressentir.

Vive à jamais, Monsieur le Général, Vive à jamais la belle et vaillante Armée Britannique !

Que Dieu donne longue vie à son Roi, à sa gracieuse Souveraine et prospérité à tout le peuple Anglais.

We leave the moment of victory and return to August 1914, when Armageddon was unloosed and the British Army first met the invader at Mons.

But, pausing in retrospect, we may rejoice that new comradeship, coming from the agony of war and the disillusion of the peace, now animates the former front-line soldiers of the nations who fought the Great War. The Silver Jubilee year, 1935, witnessed British and German ex-service men's organizations begin to work together. A delegation from the British Legion visited Germany. The Prince of Wales, himself a soldier of the Great War, in a notable speech at the Annual Conference of the British Legion, asked that " the hand of friendship " be extended to Germany. So, a new era of international relationship was begun.

CHAPTER VII

MONS AND SOISSONS

AT Mons we meet the Beginning and the End of
the Great War. At Mons, Armageddon was unloosed and the British Army [1] first met the invader.

Sunday, the 23rd August, 1914, came with its
mist, suggesting heat. The British Army was in
the field, advancing, patrols of Chetwode's cavalry
Brigade thrown out as a screen. The people
were returning from Mass, when suddenly a curtain
of fire rolled down upon them as the prelude to the
clash of steel. By 1 p.m. the Germans had entered
Mons, while, at Binche, the British Guards met the
full fury of the attack ; and soon cavalry and infantry
were engaged in a death grapple. The most remarkable feature of the Battle of Mons was its test
between two fundamentally different methods of
training infantry. The British relied on the rifle,
the Germans on the machine gun.

As at Crécy and Azincourt, each British soldier
was trained to be a marksman ; and whatever havoc
the German machine guns in defence later may have
made of British attacks, the German methods of

[1] With no precise historical exactitude this Army came to be
known as " The Contemptibles " ; and the Association of Ex-
Servicemen who served in France between August 5 and
November 22, 1914, is known as " The Old Contemptibles Association." The clasp on the 1914–15 Star is the official
recognition of this first old army.

employing infantry in these first stages of the War proved immensely costly against an army of marksmen. 130,000 Germans attacked 80,000 British soldiers. They attacked shoulder to shoulder, each Battalion in three double ranks, the rear double rank possessed of its machine guns. The German training was intended to accomplish victory by sheer weight of numbers, the machine guns to hold the position after attack. This was before the era in which was developed, with such amazing precision, indirect fire by machine guns mounted upon a fixed platform.

The French were fighting on the British right, but were in retreat. By the close of the first day more than 250,000 Germans with 920 guns were opposed to the front of the British Army with its 80,000 men and 300 guns. To the left flank, a wedge of 62,500 Germans and 230 guns was being driven in. On the road, half a million Germans and 920 guns were in pursuit of the French, leaving the British Army as a tiny isolated fortress fighting at Mons. Dusk came. The glare of burning villages and houses mounted to the skies, pigmenting the darkening gloom with all the fierce red of which Rembrandt was the master.

Those evening hours of terrible uncertainty, following a day on which the tension had never relaxed for a moment, were not surpassed in their horror when placid peace was in a moment translated into grim war, by even the most ferocious tragedies of the Somme and of Passchendaele. An army in such a position, faced with such odds, could do but one of two things, be surrounded and cut off from supplies and captured, or retreat.

The word " Retreat " is a hard one in a soldier's ears. It implies a necessity far more humiliating in its consequences than does a rearguard action or even a retirement. It means defeat. It suggests leaving the battlefield as fast as possible. If General French was to extricate his Army, it meant that men must march and march and march, day and night, marching.

Many men marched while they slept. Others dropped beside the road from sheer exhaustion. August 24th was a blazing hot day, the sun set in a cloudless sky. On this day the First Corps retired through Maubeuge, Landrecies and Maroilles, and the Second Corps to the west of Le Cateau. The men were scarcely able to drag their feet over the scorching ground. They had had nothing to eat, scarcely a moment in which they dared to stand on one side and sip water from a well-head or to pluck an apple. General von Kluck, the German Commander, forged on, victory within his grasp. But British troops cannot be driven for ever ; and there is a limit to the endurance of the British race, and then it takes its stand and fights ; and fights to the end.

At Landrecies, Maroilles and Le Cateau, the Army, exhausted beyond human endurance, hideously reduced in numbers, its men famished with hunger and thirst, many of them wounded, the ranks of Regiments reduced to but a skeleton of those who had paraded at Aldershot, their feet swathed in

bandages, stood firm. Von Kluck met a solid resistance from men who would not and could not go
farther.

The British lacerated the German attacks with
lead, stretching thousands dead on the fields.
Among flaming villages British soldiers charged with
the bayonet. Men who had not taken the saddles
from their horses' back for four days and who had
not slept charged the advancing grey hordes, hacking
and hewing with the sabre. Gunners fought their
pieces at point-blank range until the oncoming enemy
perished in the smoke before the muzzle-mouths.
In the carnage of this battlefield, refugees piled their
corpses, women and children, beside those of the
antagonists. Armageddon had been let loose, but
sheer might had not triumphed.

Four hideous years were to go by before British
troops again advanced along the roads through
Landrecies and Le Cateau. And what was left of
the dogged peasant population marched close in the
wake of the victorious British Army to view again
the homesteads which they had last seen in flames
crumpled by cannon fire.

It may be thought that there is a tendency to
over-estimate the value of the work contributed by
the small British Army at Mons and in the Retreat.
Sir John French's Force was holding a front of not
more than 20 miles in extent, while that of the
French extended over 400 miles of front, meeting
attacks of enormous strength. The eye of the
historian must necessarily go to that part of the
battlefield which presents its strategic centre ; and

beyond dispute Mons was the pivot upon which the battles of August, 1914, swung.

The German High Command were directing the blows directly on Paris. South Belgium and Picardy formed the high-road for such an operation. In order to secure the immediate success which Germany anticipated, a series of victories, culminating with the capture of Paris, were essential, and for this purpose the greatest strength of Germany was concentrated in the Armies of von Kluck and von Bülow, while the flower of the German Army was contained in the Regiments which threw themselves against the tiny British force. The assistance of the French saved this Army from complete annihilation, though the rapidity of the retreat and the strength of the final stand when men could move no farther testify to the fact that French's Army was a self-contained force, fighting its own battles in its own way against the spearhead of the German attack.

Exactly a week after the first engagement, at 4 p.m. on Sunday, 30th August, what remained of the British Army was concentrated near St. Quentin at the village of Estrees. Here were witnessed the most extraordinary scenes. The remnants of battalions and cavalry squadrons inextricably mixed with stragglers, lorries, transport waggons, guns, refugees and wounded. Two or three miles away were the German hosts. Had a Battery been brought into action before the Little Army shook itself out into some kind of formation there is little doubt that it would have been wiped out.

The Army Staff had been unable to keep touch with events ; and sometimes, as it was with General Smith-Dorrien, Corps Commanders were leading platoons and troops of cavalry. It was impossible to remain at Estrees, and orders were issued to retreat, retreat . . . keep moving. The wounded had been gathered in St. Quentin ; and such cases as were movable were again placed in ambulances and upon any kind of vehicle available and the dreadful procession of wearied, drooping men, amid them mere ghosts swathed in bloody bandages, moved on. Behind the retreating Army trees were felled, and everywhere along the roadsides, stragglers sank down in utter exhaustion, and horses which could move no farther were cut from the traces and turned adrift.

The retreat continued day after day, without sleep, without rest. Men turned and fought and then plodded on to save themselves, to save the Army. The German advance was pressed with amazing rapidity ; but it is always easier to advance with success within the grasp than it is to retire with defeat as a constant dread.

Thursday, 27th August, presented Battalions reduced from a thousand strong to not more than two hundred. The troops were in a pitiable condition, bearded and begrimed with five awful days of fierce fighting and endless marching. Their feet were swollen, sometimes bare, sometimes wound around with puttees. They were hungry, and each hour of the midday heat maddened with its thirst. Saturday morning, the 29th, found the Army still retiring. The danger of French's force may be gathered from the fact that the British base at Le Havre was evacuated, and stores and hospitals were rushed down to St. Nazaire at the mouth of the River Loire. By Sunday the retreating Army had passed through Compiègne and Soissons. Beside Compiègne on the 1st September, the action of L Battery of the Royal Horse Artillery is an epic in the history of the Royal Regiment of Artillery. The Battery was fought to the last man and the last round of ammunition; and then men wounded, some of them mortally, brought six guns out of action in the face of terrific fire. The Army took its stand on the Marne, where Marshal Joffre turned defeat into a notable victory. Even did the British Army advance again, capturing prisoners, guns and great quantities of stores. Not only was Paris saved, but the Channel ports were saved. No story in the military history of the British race is more luminous with individual acts of conspicuous gallantry and noble self-sacrifice than is the Retreat from Mons. Nor in the history of the world is there recorded any action by any body of men in which are exceeded the qualities of discipline, loyalty, endurance, patience and comradeship.

The city of Mons has been swept again and again by war. In this respect it is not unlike the city of Ypres. But in former years Ypres had suffered no destruction, while Mons had been sacked and burned. During the Great War, Ypres was reduced to brick-dust, but Mons suffered no hurt from the passage of troops, or from the battles which were fought around the city.

Mons, with more than 27,000 inhabitants, is at the centre of a rich mining and agricultural district, and is a city of most ancient foundation. Its castle was built under the Roman Empire and is called the Château-Caesar. Belgium has always been the cock-pit of Europe, and Mons has shared largely in that fate. The old monastery was destroyed in 1283 by invaders of Thierry. The celebrated procession of Mons each year on the 7th October commemorates the relief of the city from plague in 1349. The first siege of Mons was that of 1425 under Jacqueline of Bavaria. In the fourteenth century the city rose to distinction as a centre for the textile trade, but the religious wars of the sixteenth century reduced its prosperity to obscurity.

. . . Taken by the French and relieved in the fifteenth century, Mons remained a centre of contention. Louis XIV brought fresh calamities to the city ; but during the long siege in the year 1678, in which the inhabitants fought valiantly against the French Army and made frequent vigorous sorties, it was relieved on the 14th August. Again assailed by the French with an army of 80,000 men in 1691, Louis XIV seized the city on the 10th April and made a triumphal entry. Mons remained under the suzerainty of France until 1697, and again in 1701 the French reoccupied it. But after his victory at Malplaquet, Marlborough with his allies besieged the city in 1709 and forced it to capitulate. In 1713, under the terms of the Treaty of Utrecht, Mons was placed under the domination of Austria. Besieged again by Louis XIV in 1746, the French

SCAR 77

By

GRAHAM SETON

(Lieut.-Col. Graham Seton Hutchison)

Author of "The 'W' Plan"

"Marked men, a secret society, a plot to ruin the British Empire.... From El Arish to Prague, from Prague to the Cataract of Shabluka, Allamdollillah, Arabs, Zaharofs, an anxious C.I.G.S., hidden agents, a beautiful dancer, and finally, Colonel Duncan Grant of the 'W' Plan.... All woven together in a bewildering tangle of excitements and hair-breadth adventures. What is it all about? What is the clue? Who are the numbered men? And who is SCAR 77? I cannot tell you without reading to you this book, so you must read it for yourselves." *Major-Gen. J. F. C. Fuller.*

7s. 6d.

RICH & COWAN, LTD.
25 SOHO SQUARE, LONDON, W.1

AN UNDERGROUND CASUALTY CLEARING STATION, ARRAS

Professor Henry Tonks.

A RED CROSS TRAIN, FRANCE

H. Septimus Power.

captured the city and demolished its fortifications. But by the Peace of Aix-la-Chapelle in 1748, Mons was again returned to Austria. In the subsequent wars the French took and evacuated the town time after time. Reunited within the French Empire, Mons became the capital of the Department of Jemappes until 1814; and it was not until after the final defeat of Napoleon by British and German Armies that Mons enjoyed a hundred years of uninterrupted peace, until diplomatic disregard, financial and economic rivalry and ambitions again made Belgium the cock-pit of a war which has been curiously termed " the great war for civilization."

Mons preserved many ancient and beautiful monuments. Of these the Hôtel de Ville, with its curious sculptures, and the Château de Monceau on the River Sambre are fine examples of mediæval architecture, and contain fine specimens of the paintings of the great artists of the Flemish School, Rubens, Otto van Veen, Van Thulden and other masters. The belfry, styled the " tour du château," is the only example of seventeenth-century baroque architecture in Belgium and its foundation was laid in 1662. It is a sad commentary upon the city of Mons and the district which surrounds it that a large proportion of the inhabitants to-day are stunted in growth, and ill-equipped, as it would seem, to carry forward the ancient traditions of the city. Modern civilization, with its immense resources for making possible the recuperation of a population, may succeed where apparently a long interval of peace failed to raise the morale of the

L

population. Following the Great War, earnest men of all nations seem to have been turning their eyes towards the ennoblement of the human race. Even war and battle, with their immense sacrifices and losses, rather than debasing the character of men, as the epic story of the Retreat from Mons clearly establishes, called from them the highest qualities of character and demanded the exhibition of the most noble virtues. If the soldier has disappeared from leadership, the statesman of peace, in an age of incomparable plenty and possibility for leisure, has an enormous responsibility. The Old Contemptibles with neither plenty nor leisure showed what British determination can do. The modern statesman with untold resources can do no less.

The Retreat from Mons fell back towards Paris, halting on the River Aisne, and then on the Marne. The city of Soissons became the centre of a battle-field, upon which some of the fiercest duels of the Great War were fought out. The Battles of the Aisne and of the Marne are historic. The latter ranks perhaps with those of Malplaquet, Compiègne, Minden, Gettysburg, perhaps even Waterloo. Château Thierry, Berry-au-bac and the Chemin des Dames witnessed not only some of the fiercest fighting of the Great War, but that also of the most profound strategic significance. Soissons, forty miles from Paris, is almost the last stronghold along its road from the east.

The city is remarkably picturesque and bears a venerable aspect. It is best seen from the meadows on the right flank of the Aisne. Everywhere there

re pleasant walks, redolent with the scent of limes
1 the late spring, while the streets are full of quaint
haracter. The Cathedral of Nôtre Dame is a very
erfect and magnificent Gothic church, its founda-
.ons begun at the end of the twelfth century and
nished at the close of the thirteenth. The noble
ose window, the open gallery above it, and the
ower with statues at the angles have been faithfully
reserved; while one authority, Farguersson, tells
s in regard to the choir, dating from 1212, that
nothing can exceed the justness of the proportions
f the centre and side aisles, both in themselves
nd to one another." Once at Soissons was the
nagnificent abbey of St. Jean des Vignes, where
'homas à Becket lived in 1170; but long before
he War it had fallen into ruins and little remained
ut its façade. In the early history of France
here were Kings of Soissons, and Clotaire I was
ere proclaimed in the sixth century. He is buried
1 the abbey of St. Medard, a short distance from the
ity on the right bank of the Aisne.

The notable victory of the Marne was essentially
'rench. The claims of Marshal Joffre to recognition
est indubitably upon the stand of the French Army
1 its historic battle of September, 1914. The
iritish Army, reduced during the retreat almost
o insignificance, played a glorious part, its hungry,
wearied troops returning to the attack with an élan
which astonished the French, with whom they fought
houlder to shoulder.

The wars of earlier history, especially those of
Marlborough, had exposed the difficulties, jealousies,

misunderstandings which inevitably arise betwee
allies of different nations even when fighting
common battle for a common cause. There wer
recriminations between the High Commands whic
permeated to the meanest camp follower, and pa
no doubt of the German success, and the failur
of the Allies, notably in 1914, on the Somme i
1916, and during the German offensive in 191⁸
can be traced to the lack of cohesion in the Allie
Army, even to an absence of fraternal feelings an
of mutual confidence. Yet it is of extraordinar
interest and of even more profound significance tha
the essential unity of purpose and mutual confidenc
between British and French Armies were discovere
in the deepest agony of the Soissons battlefiel
when weakened and almost defeated soldiers, in
extricably mixed together, received the hammer blow
of the Germans before the gates of Paris, and ofte
completely surrounded by the hordes of the enem
died together in isolated posts, fighting to the las
man and to the last round of ammunition. Th
epic fights of the five British Divisions, marchin
within the French Army, were the foundation of th
astonishing series of victories under the suprem
command of Marshal Foch, which within fou
short months turned defeat into the most astonishin
climax of triumph which the world has eve
witnessed.

The fair pastures, woods and vales betwee
Soissons and the city of Rheims are soaked wit
blood. Not only were here fought out the battl
whose names are noted, but on the heights of th

Chemin des Dames, General Nivelle, in an awful experiment between the 15th April and the 15th May, 1917, hurled an immense French force, which on its first day perished hopelessly before the German barbed wire and machine-gun emplacements. So tremendous was the slaughter, so devastating the defeat, that the French Army, lacking all confidence in its command, largely mutinied, and thousands of them refused to take any further part in the War. A thick veil of secrecy was drawn over all that transpired, nor has it any place here. The fact remains that under the leadership of Marshal Pétain and of Marshal Foch, the French Army rallied, and played not only a glorious part in the supreme test at Soissons a year later, but poured out its blood for the liberation of France from the invader in the succeeding months.

CHAPTER VIII

THE AISNE AND THE MARNE

Former wars—Mercenaries—Scots and Irish—Lions in the field, lambs in the house—Soissons, 1918—The American contribution— Chemin des Dames taken, 1918—County regiments.

IN thinking of mediæval history, one is inclined to assume that battles of such historic significance as were, for example, those of Azincourt or Malplaquet were fought between nations and allied nations. But this is far from the truth. The first national war of any importance was that of 1870–71, between France and Germany. Those of the mediæval ages were feudal. The student, without a broad sense of history, conceives of Azincourt as being a contest between England and France; or of the contests which again and again swept over Ypres and Mons as being battles between France and Belgium. This was not so. The sense of nationality is of comparatively recent growth. Germany was not a nation until Bismarck made it so. France was divided between the great dukedoms, those, for example, of Normandy, Burgundy, Orleans, which sometimes acknowledged the suzerainty of the King of France in Paris or were in alliance with him. But often the Kings of France were beset with wars in which the lesser princes, knights, and feudal serfs of some great overlord were arrayed against him. Napoleon gave birth to the French national sense of which La Marseillaise is the echo.

The Kings of England, as late as the eighteenth

century, possessed territories on the Continent and their subjects gave to them their unswerving allegiance. English Kings were frequently at war with the Scottish chieftains and their clansmen; and in the Lowlands of Scotland there were English barons in their castles who commanded the loyalty of men of Scottish blood, though most frequently they were not also of Celtic descent. Marlborough commanded an army of Englishmen and of citizens of what is now known as Belgium, Germany and Luxembourg; and his storm troops were Hessians. The common soldier felt no loyalty to a country, though he possessed a love for his own soil. Translated into terms of patriotism, such loyalty could only be given to the seigneur in the manor, to the knight in the château, and perhaps to the princes living in the city, in whose gift also were the benefices of the great abbeys. To understand history, therefore, and to appreciate the novelty of the World War, it is necessary to realize the historic growth of nationalism, from the family group up the scale, until great nations were fashioned set behind political frontiers. Just as the French Kings found it convenient to foster alliances with the Kings and Chiefs of Scotland so that England would not be entirely free to harry the northern coast of France, but would be preoccupied also with the bother of invasion from the north, so also the new nations established alliances one with another for mutual security.

Point is given to these observations from the history of Scotland.

Even so far back as the twelfth century, Scotsmen protected the French Kings, and for three or four centuries later the " Scottish Guard " was always famed for its devotion. It continued to be a feature of the French Court, defending the sovereigns with great valour at Liège, at Proia, and elsewhere, and at length came over to England, and under its leader, Hepburn, adopted the Royal cause in the troubles which ultimately brought the head of Charles I to the block. Loyal to the last, the Scots then returned to France and resumed their position as part of the guard of Louis XIV. " The Scotch," says Henry Torrens, " have ever held a high military reputation throughout Europe." Froissart, who, with his usual accuracy, describes the habits of their border troops, speaks of them as bold, hardy and much inured to war in a national sense. They became individually esteemed as soldiers by their early practice of leaving their native land to seek service and fortune on the Continent of Europe. From the days of Louis XI of France to the Thirty Years' War (1617–48), the valour, coolness and probity of the Scottish soldier continued to rise to higher and higher estimation in every land in which he took service; and it is remarkable that, in spite of the alleged national acquisitiveness, he has, by his honourable conduct, entirely escaped the reproach (*Point d'argent, point de Suisse*) which has attached itself to another celebrated free nation whose mercenaries have cut each other's throats hereditarily in every army in Europe for the last five centuries.

In 1709 the Greys formed part of the troops covering the siege and fall of Tournay; but the event of the year was Malplaquet, fought on September 11, 1709. The Greys were brigaded with the Royal Irish Dragoons, under Brigadier-General Sybourg. They were posted near the centre of the allied army to sustain the attacks of the infantry and protect the artillery, and for some time were only spectators of the fierce storm of battle which raged on all sides; at length, however, they were ordered to file through a wood in their front, and charge. Scarcely had the brigade emerged from among the trees before it encountered a line of French cavalry; these squadrons were, however, soon dispersed, but they were instantly succeeded by a new line of champions, consist-

ing of a number of squadrons of the French Household
Cavalry, clad in armour, and advancing in firm array. . . .
The Greys and Irish Dragoons met these foaming
squadrons with signal bravery, but were driven from
their ground by superior numbers. The two regiments
soon rallied, and being joined by several corps of horse,
returned to the charge; yet such was the resolution displayed by the French troopers that it was not until the
third charge that they were driven from the field. The
two victorious regiments were specially thanked by the
Duke of Marlborough. The Greys lost about thirty
killed and wounded.

In writing of the Scots, whose contribution in
the Great War, great as it was, must not be exaggerated or exhibited in a disproportionate light, it must
be remembered that for centuries France and
Flanders had grown accustomed to their presence as
" valiant " allies, men spoke of " *L'alliance ancienne*."
Continental opinion of the Highlander-in-arms was
by tradition very high long before 1914.

In Antwerp much was said of the Highlanders. A
gentleman had, when the wounded arrived, been recognized and spoken to by a poor Highlander. The circumstance absolutely gave him a kind of consideration in the
crowd; he felt prouder at the moment than if a prince
had smiled upon him. At Brussels, and everywhere in
the Netherlands, when the English troops were mentioned,
whom they likewise much admired, the natives always
returned to the Scotch with—" But the Scotch, they are
good and kind, as well as brave; they are the only soldiers
who become members of the family in the houses in which
they are billeted; they even carry about the children and
do the domestic work." The favourite proverbial form
of compliment was, " Lions in the field and lambs in the
house." There was a competition among the inhabitants
who should have them in their houses; and when they
returned wounded, the same house they had left had its

doors open, and the family went out some miles to meet
" our own Scotsman." The people had many instances
to relate of the generosity of these men ; after the battle
many, although themselves wounded, were seen binding
up the wounds of the French and assisting them with
their arm. On the contrary, it is well known that very
few of our soldiers fell into the hands of the enemy without being murdered in cold blood. There cannot be a
better test of two nations, a more satisfactory decision of
the question on which the peace and happiness of mankind
should depend.

Here, on the battlefields of the Chemin des
Dames, the Aisne and the Marne, soaked with the
blood of thousands of Frenchmen, France learned
through an alliance and a supreme test of arms, in
which English troops were for France " our own
Englishmen," to estimate them at the highest value.
Two English Territorial Battalions received as
Battalions the rare and coveted distinction of the
Croix de Guerre with the Palm. In the official
French report occurs this generous sentence. ' *L'im-
pression produite sur le moral des troupes françaises
par la belle attitude de leurs alliés a été très bonne.*"

These British Divisions now before Soissons had
borne already a full share of the terrific fighting on
the Somme and on the Lys. The intention was
that they should occupy a quiet section of the line,
while reorganizing with new officers and men, few
of whom had any previous experience of war. They
were thrust into the line north of the Aisne on the
fateful Chemin des Dames.

Germany, baffled after the hammer blows on the
Somme and on the Lys, was by no means dismayed.
The Allies were badly shaken. By some critics the

strategy of Ludendorff had been subjected to sharp criticism. The apparent indetermination of gigantic assaults first upon one part of the front and then upon another, Somme, Lys, Kemmel, without the capture of the prized objectives, is perhaps misinterpreted. However much the optimism of the German General Staff permitted it to be prodigal in loss of men, not only was the moment chosen supremely opportune, but the losses inflicted on an already weakened enemy were immense. And if the great objectives which strategic considerations determined as being most desirable were denied by the resistance, Germany zealously played the allied game of a war of attrition; and was almost successful. Weighing all the probabilities, that Germany failed must, by the historian, be attributed to the entry of American troops upon the field of battle.

> Take up our quarrel with the foe!
> To you from failing hands we throw
> The torch—be yours to hold it high!
> If ye break faith with us who die,
> We shall not sleep, though poppies grow
> In Flanders fields.[1]

The contribution of the United States of America on the Western Front must essentially be regarded from two entirely different standpoints, namely political and strategic on the one hand, and the tactical effort and actual fighting on the other. It does not belittle the military qualities of the American Divisions who participated in battle when it is stated that their contribution in the fighting zone

[1] From *In Flanders Fields*, by Colonel John McCrae.

was of comparatively small importance. Operations like those of St. Mihiel and in conjunction with British troops against the Hindenburg Line, successful in degree as they were, cannot be pretended to have exercised any marked influence upon the progress of the War or upon the defeat of Germany. The battles on the Western Front between August and the Armistice would have proceeded according to plan, and doubtless would have accomplished the same objectives, whether American troops had been present or not. That is the tactical consideration, but, paradoxically, and in apparent contradiction, it is equally clear that without the presence of American troops it is improbable that the Allied Drive would have proceeded as it did. And it is still more doubtful whether the Armistice, following collapse, would have intervened to prevent a further winter campaign, and a war of considerably longer duration. That is the consideration of strategy.

The importance of the moral factor bound up with America's entry into the War on the Allied side can hardly be over-estimated. The appearance of fresh and eager troops, filled with self-confidence, well equipped, and of fine physique, provided the Allies with a stimulus beyond compare. Those familiar with military history, also, were confident that the successors to those who with such skill and courage had conducted the campaigns of the American Civil War, although lacking training and experience of modern conditions, would prove to be troops of the highest fighting quality.

What the Allies realized in the attachment of America, instructed opinion in Germany understood as a weight beyond counterbalance thrown into the scales against the chance, severely diminished after April, 1918, for the Central Powers of bringing the War to a successful conclusion. American opposition, even with the restraint of President Wilson's enunciation as to the political objective sought, deprived Germany of any but the most slender hopes of an agreed peace. The advent of American troops, both on account of the untold numbers which America could produce, and of the stimulus provided among the Allies, brought defeat on the battlefield very close to war-weary German soldiers, so that it stared them in the face.

The influence of America was, therefore, a moral one. Nor can it be too often repeated that " in war moral force is to physical as is three to one." That so few Americans were called upon to play any active part in battle is no cause for minimizing the part which they did play ; nor long after the Armistice for a querulous criticism of bombastic claims made in some quarters that " America won the War."

In a strategic sense it cannot be denied that the entry of the United States on the Allied side was the decisive factor. It gave heart to France, when among the Allies the French politicians especially were very doubtful of the possibility of success to their arms ; and when the British, greatly exhausted from the German hammer blows of March and April, 1918, though not discouraged by their great losses in a stand which must be regarded as a success for British arms, were neither equipped nor were in a mood for further offensive action. France was willing to " sit tight "; Great Britain could do no more. Germany, having suffered prodigious losses, felt the urgent need of a shorter defensive line, and was prepared to evacuate a large part of the invaded territory in order to accomplish this object; and then to " dig in " and treat for peace, one which would be agreed.

The entry of the Americans contributed to Marshal Foch the lever which his strategic belief required, indeed a flail with which to goad forward both doubting politicians and wary subordinates. " *Marcher aux canons* " became a possibility only because young America, a child in war, youthfully adventuresome in its personnel, was the whip which Foch showmanship could crack to encourage the Allied troops to perform their old tricks, and which terrified the growling enemy across the dividing bars of the trenches.

America did not win the War by any feat of arms, but by the presence of her troops in France and by the threat of a million more to come. America accomplished the Armistice as much through Wilson's " Fourteen Points " as by the fact of placing a million fresh combatants at the disposal of the Allies. The effect of the publication of the " Fourteen Points " in Germany upon German soldiers could only be estimated long after the Armistice. Their impression, with profound reverberations, only began to suggest to the world so long as a decade later that, in the " Peace Terms," Germany had expected something different from an Allied interpretation of those Points. They were a main cause of Germany's laying down arms, but it is difficult to find them as implemented in the Treaty of Versailles.

But the " Fourteen Points" no less than the entry of American troops in the field, provided Foch with additional strength to wield his whip, once he had crossed the fortified Hindenburg Line and strode in among an enemy which, though yet growling, retreated before his blows. In the realm of strategy the American entry, with the portent of its " Fourteen Points," embraced at the time by the Allies, was the factor decisive of victory. Thus the power of moral force.

To return to the Aisne, as did Germany with the smashing blow of the 27th May. Four British Divisions, the 50th Northumbrian from the north of England ; the 8th, steeped in the war traditions of its famous battalions, on the right ; the 21st astride the Aisne in the Berry au Bac Sector ; and the 25th Division in reserve at Fisnes—these were acting as part of the French Army, and held a front of about eight miles. It would not be possible to follow the fortunes of each Division, though the detailed history is everywhere luminous with acts of astonishing gallantry and self-sacrifice.

The position on the Chemin des Dames was always endangered by the river in the rear. But the French would not evacuate the Chemin des Dames and the famous California Plateau beside Craonne, wrested from the enemy at such tremendous cost in the previous year. Just before dawn on the 27th May, a shattering bombardment of the whole area between Soissons and Rheims began. So thoroughly was the complement of gas shells mixed with high explosive that in addition to the levelling of the trenches, the zone of attack behind the Allied line was soaked in gas to a depth of eight miles. The British were weak in artillery and could scarcely reply to the onslaught. The Germans, massed in woods, suddenly debouched, following the bombardment. Utilizing the clever " infiltration tactics " which they had perfected, and which had superseded the mass assaults that had characterized the attack in 1914 over this ground, they poured through the thinly held lines, delivering the offensive also with extraordinary determination and courage.

By 5 a.m. British Battalions were surrounded, fighting, front and rear, left and right flank, against overwhelming odds. At Craonne the 150th Brigade of Yorkshiremen met the full fury of the attack. On the left of the British line, and on the right of the French 118th Regiment, in a moment it was literally swept away, commanding officers fighting tooth and claw at the point of the pistol among their perishing platoons. The French resistance here was annihilated. In a house in the village of Craonnelle, the Commander of the 4th Yorks with sixteen men held out until all were killed or wounded. But this was typical of what occurred along the whole of the Chemin des Dames and the bridgeheads of the Aisne. For the third time within nine weeks the Germans had delivered a great blow against the Allies, wresting from them the whole of the ground gained during the previous three years, and paling the successes of the Somme, Ypres and the Chemin des Dames to insignificance. Not that the costs had not been high : German casualties within the thirteen weeks which encompassed the great offensives of March, April, May on the Western Front amounted to 688,000 men, against the British 16,000 officers and 419,000 men and against the French 253,000 officers and men.

The remnant of the British Divisions fell back. Some idea of their prodigious losses may be formed from the fact that the 8th Division alone suffered a loss of 7,000 men from the total force of some 9,000 infantry.

On the morning of the 29th a new British Division, the 19th, arrived from rest to an urgent summons. French and British Divisions were intermixed and mixed, suffering the very real difficulty of difference in language, attempting to shake themselves out south of Fisnes. Soissons had fallen, Rheims was in imminent danger. The 19th Division was composed of boys fresh from English and Welsh training camps ; and into a breach between the 13th French Division at Lhery and the 154th Division near Faverolles, this little bit of England was thrust to meet the ordeal of battle.

The 19th Division became the fighting front. The Germans let loose the new attack at dawn on May 30th. Lhery fell, while the 10th Worcester-

M

shires lost sixty per cent. of its men and all its officers. Yet this Division continued to hold a front of 12,000 yards. Retreating step by step, sometimes delivering a local counter-attack, the Division was forced back. By the 31st May not one of the three Brigades could muster 1,000 rifles, while that in reserve had been reduced to 350 men, a bare ten per cent. of its fighting strength.

As the situation became graver, as the losses piled themselves up, as defeat stared the defenders more certainly in the face, a bond of comradeship between British and French soldiers, wholly dissimilar from the vagueness of an alliance, was suddenly summoned to their aid, a bond which contributed to the shattered and tottering defence its indestructible cohesion.

At a critical period a company of the 10th Gloucesters, vainly attempting by counter-attack to regain the high ground north of Chambrecy, was joined by the 22nd French Regiment, led in person by its Commandant, de Lasbourde, and then assisted by the 10th Worcestershires. The result was a startling victory, perhaps only of minute local importance, but whose moral consequence was immense.

The furious attacks continued with the utmost determination and the highest courage, but the staggering defence stiffened, even at the moment when it appeared to be well-nigh overwhelmed.

The German attack was held.

The emphasis attributed to the achievements of Scottish troops during the War has been noticed. A reason may be that many journalists are Scotsmen: and the distinctive uniform of the Scot invites description of the picturesque, while also the peculiar character of the Scot exhibits itself most favourably in the dramatic action of attack rather than in the less inviting picture of defence under conditions of modern warfare. The exploits of one Regiment of English soldiers are typical of the contribution of England throughout the War. The action of the 2nd Battalion Worcestershires at Gheluvelt is one of the finest in the annals of the British race. The defence of Neuve Église Church and *Mairie* in April, 1918, is an epic comparable with the stand at Waterloo and of Rorke's Drift. The survivors of the 10th Battalion of this Regiment with A/88 Battery R.F.A., formed a last line of defence on the crest of Messines Ridge on the 10th April, 1918, a feat of arms and a display of dogged courage which have never been surpassed. Only a month later this same Battalion withstood the shock of the fiercest assaults of the Germans before Soissons. As at Neuve Église and Messines, while the French cried " *Ils ne passeront pas!* " the Worcestershires set a limit beyond which the advance of the German storm troops should not go.

The River Aisne passes through the city of Soissons. Left and right of the river, and following the line of the Chemin des Dames, lie some thirty cemeteries in which rest the bones of Englishmen who fought shoulder to shoulder with their French comrades and discovered the Comradeship of Battle.

CHAPTER IX

THE PILGRIM AT YPRES

National pride—British characteristics—Common purpose—Strategic
importance of Ypres—Every belligerent nation represented—The
cockpit of Europe—Flemish character.

As the pilgrim or traveller passes across the battlefields of Flanders and Picardy, unless he be dead to
the virtues and characteristics to which his homeland
has given birth, and which generation after generation have been nurtured therein, he will look here
and there for Memorials to those of his own country,
his town or district.

He may find a focus for his reflections in some
noble stone or bronze monument, or it may be in
some solitary grave in a cemetery, isolated from the
whirlpool of the battles. But instinctively a thrill
of pride will surge through his veins as he beholds
the monument of sacrifice to those of his own flesh
and blood, to a kith and kin, who in a not very
remote history would have been the playmates of
his youth, his neighbours and bound to him by family
ties or friendship. And in the cemetery, his gaze
arrested by the name of some Regiment, denoting
the territory of his ancestors, he will stoop to read
the inscription and again will be sensible of some
common ideal and purpose between himself and him
who sacrificed a life that this purpose should be
served.

But a century ago, the peoples of the British Isles
were men of the land. The era of industrialism
had not yet herded them into cities, wherein super-

ficially it may seem that they have lost characteristics which in such marked fashion stamp those who tread the soil of the open spaces. The idea of nation is of recent growth : that of village, of vale, of moor and lake, of town and of county reaches back to the beginnings of history. Nothing will persuade the yeomen of Dorset or of Suffolk that their characteristics are the same as those of London Cockneys or of the Welsh. Even the very phraseology of a common language with its varied dialects denotes a difference of character obvious to the observer.

It is the nature of the countryside, seaboard and woods, stone and heather, rich loam and pasture, chill northern blasts or warm southern coves, which through the centuries has produced a stock as various as is the countryside of Britain. Nor is the Scot an Englishman, nor the Irish anything but a man of Ireland. The Welsh, with a carefully preserved tongue, remain a distinct people. A memorial to the Welsh cries from the heart of Wales : the graven stone above the bones of a man from the Border Regiment reincarnates for the imagination the fells of Cumberland. In some districts of England men speak slowly, weighing their words, from a deep wisdom, discovered in the open spaces. The language of the London Cockney piles word on word, quick, witty, jostling like the people in the streets of the great city. The Scot is often dour as are his misty braes and grey skies ; but this sadness is often pierced with shafts of wit even as the skies are gashed by sunlight. The men of the South-western Counties of England appear slow to the citizen of the Northern commercial city; but these are the men who have given strength to the beleaguered trench and have been the wall which so long as one brick stood in its place could not be passed. The Highlander, striding across the knee-deep heather, is long of limb and big of bone, accustomed to long journeys and to facing the caprice of the elements. He was swift, determined and terrible in the attack. Each district of England breeds a different type of man; the men of the Lowlands of Scotland vary from the Celtic Highlander; the Cornish fishermen have little in common with the shipbuilders of Tyneside except the pursuit of the sea.

As this is true of Britain, it is noteworthy also of France, of Germany, of Italy and of every nation in the world. " *Pour la France !* " in the last century may have summoned men as a nation to defend a common frontier; but the Breton is not the Basque; the fair-haired men of Normandy and Picardy have little in common with the swarthy Marseillard or with the mountaineers of the Savoy. Germany, whose national unity dates only from the era of Bismarck, is composed of Prussians and Hanoverians, of Saxons and Bavarians, of Hessians and of races whose structure and characteristics throughout past history have shown them as always various. And this is true of Italy, wherein, for example, the citizens of Naples are so different from those of Piedmont.

One may think of the common purpose of a nation, of its racial origins, of its contribution towards the culture of the world, of the factors which contribute to its cohesion; but one must always be conscious of the fact that though nationality is determined always by common racial origin and language, sometimes by economic and political forces, it is the valley, the lake, the seaport with its surroundings, the moorland expanse, indeed the very configuration of land and quality of soil, which express through the people their varied characteristics.

To some men, London, with its endless streets, its lights and sounds, its vast population and its throbbing industry, is home. To others it is anathema, or at most but a centre of entertainment and business and from which to escape. Some must view the wind-swept moors of Yorkshire or peer down into the lakes of Westmoreland in order to experience that strange kinship with soil and stone and tree and of human habitation which men call home. Others must hear the Welsh tongue spoken or the soft accents of Devonshire; and others, with the view of glen and burn beneath the black mountains, must be able to murmur " O Caledonia ! stern and wild."

Each Memorial, each Cemetery and every grave awakens the sense of home.

The time will never come when men will become so unmindful of their history and traditions and of the special qualities which by some Divine purpose Nature has contributed to their race, that they will forget the land of their birth and the vales and villages which bore their forefathers.

Though the territory of Belgium was of immense

political significance at the outbreak of the Great War and throughout—the faint line of hills west of Ypres covering the Channel ports were of great strategic importance—in fact, only a corner of the Kingdom witnessed the fighting. But what fighting!

Ypres and its close surround is the graveyard of no less than one million men. Enemy, occupying all Belgium but a strip of Flanders, governed the Belgian people, while the soldier King, Albert I, remained the sovereign of their hearts. Germany sacked and burned Louvain, one of the most beautiful cities in the world, an act of folly which no cruel necessity of war could excuse. Even so, the comment of Winston Churchill, whose historical insight is so remarkable, justly cynical, is here not without significance.

Of course, nowadays, with the many improvements that have been made in international morals and behaviour, all enemy subjects, even those whose countries were only technically involved, even those who had lived their lives in England, and the English women who had married them, would, as in every other state based on an educated democracy, be treated within twenty-four hours as malignant foes, flung into internment camps, and their private property stolen to assist the expenses of the war. In the twentieth century mankind has shaken itself free from all those illogical, old-world prejudices, and achieved the highest efficiency of brutal, ruthless war.[1]

British, French and American soldiers all fought in Flanders, and scarcely one Division in the German Army did not witness the gruesome battlefields around Ypres. The remnant of the Belgian Army,

[1] *Marlborough, his Life and Times*, Vol. II.

some 80,000 men in all, led by their King, fought
back step by step, holding on to the western fringe
of their country, and there they remained, between
Lombartzyde and Houthulst Forest, through the
War, for the most part leading an amphibious exist-
ence amid the Inundations. But in October, 1918,
the Belgian Army was rearmed to play its forward
part with the great Allied Armies.

Britons, more than any others, saw much of
Flemish character between 1914 and 1919, and
were continually astonished by its complexities.
Ethnographically, Flanders extends beyond the definition of its political frontier ; and in the Middle
Ages the Grand Pagus de la Menapie, the province
which embraced that of Flandre, was bounded on
the west by a frontier which ran through St. Omer,
Aire and then turned east following the course of
the River Lys. Belgium, in its various historical
epochs, has suffered much from the invader. The
inhabitants are of both French origin, as around
Mons, and of Flemish stock, a distinct race. To
create a homogeneous Belgian nation has always,
therefore, been the supreme difficulty in political
life. King Albert, through the power of his zealous
courageous patriotism and his immaculate life,
alone achieved Belgium's absolute unity. Throughout history the invader succeeded always in dividing
the inhabitants of the Belgian provinces, and broadly,
the French and the Flemish can divide their
sympathies between those who struggled for
supremacy of their soil, those of French origin
attaching themselves as was natural to the French,

the Flemish to the Germans. Romans, Spaniards, Austrians ruled over the Belgian provinces until the French Revolution and the Napoleonic era. The Belgians writhed under " a brutal administration " of the past Revolutionary period, and a " great number of the conscripted militia, refusing to serve the detested government, hiding themselves in the forests." [1]

The Treaty of London, 1815, following the Congress of Vienna, amalgamated Belgium and Holland as the Royaume des Pays-Bas. But the Belgian Provinces revolted against William of Orange, and by the new Treaty, signed in 1831, Belgium attained its independence, the National Congress nominating Prince Leopold of Saxe-Coburg, grandfather of King Albert I, as the first Sovereign. To assess the character of a people, divided by race, language and custom, who have been subjected so continually to alien control, in whole or in part, is difficult. Except for brief periods at Mons in 1914 and again in 1918, contact was made by British troops alone with the Flemish. The Flemish tongue is very akin to German, a factor always useful to the German soldiery. To the average English soldier, his ear crudely, or in the higher ranks more or less, accustomed to French words, the Flemish tongue was baffling. The River Lys is indicated by the Italian authority, Villani, as the linguistic frontier—

" Liscia, ovesi parte la lingua Francesca dalla Fiaminga." [2]

---

[1] *Dictionnaire Historique et Géographique des Communes Belges,* Eugène de Seyn, Vol. I, pp. 36–37.

[2] *Histoire Florentine,* Voltaire.

The origins of the Belgian people, together with the varied influences which have governed them throughout the long centuries, have produced, therefore, a most complex character. Belgium is also the most densely inhabited country in the world, its population being concentrated in the industrial zones. Whatever may eventuate, a marked cleavage in outlook between the farmers and peasants on the one hand and those engaged in big industry on the other is to be noticed. A strong nationalism did not exist in the Belgium of past history ; and except under the leadership of the late King Albert, who focused it in his own personality, it has never been apparent. Yet, strangely, amid these clashes of culture perhaps the world's greatest school of painting arose, as did music in Austria, where Teutonic, Latin, Slav and Czech cultures meet.

British troops made contact with the Flemish peasants almost alone. They are dour in demeanour, hard-working, independent and reserved. They regarded the invasion, whether by British or German soldiers, as a monstrous interference with their liberties, as indeed it was ; nor was this impression mitigated as the War dragged on. The trumpeted victories of British Armies gave them no relief whatever ; while the last straw which broke the back of their patience was the retreat in the valley of the Lys and the loss of Mont Kemmel in April, 1918, wherefrom the last cultivated acres of a Belgian Belgium were surrendered to the enemy and to devastation by shell-fire.

The long-suffering peasants, knowing little or

nothing of what transpired along the fighting front of a world war, exiled from their flaming homesteads and battered villages, hurled their pent-up anger indiscriminately against the invader, and since they were nearest at hand, their wrath descended upon the British troops. They had never understood the British soldier, and the difficulty of language, which possessed no common ground, had always proved a formidable obstacle to the fraternization which an elementary grounding in French made possible between the British and the Picards. The Flemish, largely divested of their means of livelihood, utilized the invader for profit, and almost for profit alone. Nor is this surprising. Belgian soldiers, segregated as they were in the Inundations, made no contact with the British Armies.

Although, therefore, for Great Britain the front in Flanders was of the highest strategic importance, guarding as it did the Channel Ports and the line of communications; and although the greatest dramas of the War for Great Britain surrounded Ypres, British soldiers knew little of Belgium, and had no such opportunity to come close to the Belgian heart as they did, for example, to that of France on the Somme, at Soissons and in the villages of Artois and Picardy.

The Germans, on the other hand, despite the stern restrictions of the invasion, possessed of a language not dissimilar from Flemish, and living among a people long and even lately accustomed to foreign domination and to invading armies, experienced little difficulty in arriving at a compromise

s a ground for friendship, where both the Flemish
peasants and the front-line soldiers were in so
evil a case. And as the War continued, month by
month, year by year, the Belgian population east
of the front lines, with stoic fatalism settled themselves to the new life under foreign domination
with little interruption of its daily round. For,
after all, the civil population in, for example,
Roulières, Courtrai, Brussels or Antwerp had to
be fed, and for this the farmers, as always, were
responsible ; while the addition of hundreds of
thousands of German soldiers out of the line with
money in their pockets to be spent on small luxuries
provided a new source of revenue. But this is
not to suggest that the Belgians, whose independence
is so marked, were not glad to see the backs of the
German hosts, as they were to be relieved of the
impositions of the Allies. All of which suggests
that Belgium, which throughout the centuries has
been the " cockpit of Europe," by its own inclination
would have nothing of war.

CHAPTER X

YPRES, almost personified, spiritually if not in flesh
and blood, in its stricken tower of masonry, the
Cloth Hall. Out from the Menin Gate north-east,
east, south-east, to the extremities of the fan-shaped
Salient—Langemarck, Passchendaele, Broodseinde,
Gheluvelt, Ploegsteert. The Salient itself, pockmarked and obscene with shell-holes.

This was Ypres of the years 1914–19.

The tree-tops of Polygon Wood, or Inverness
Copse, mere splintered stumps, swift landmark
against a star-shell-lighted horizon. Roads, pitted
ugly with metal-blazed balks of timber, their sides
piled with stinking carcasses, mere tracks over which
tramp silently ten thousand men going east; and
coming west, limp and trickle as many thousand
more. Among them are horses, hairy as Highland
cattle, dragging guns axle-deep in mud across the
wasted fields and macadamless roads of Potijze or
Zonnebeke, in bitter wind and driving rain, with no
other light to brighten their journey into the unknown than the quick-cut flash of bursting cordite
or that of the fog-veiled star-shell. Those who live
and have their being in the Salient remain the
audience of a sublime orchestra, whose crescendo
of shrieking shell and thunder of guns intermittently
thrills and appals, and whose pianissimo of distant

178

cry coming over the sky-line at dawn lulls them to fitful slumber.

How we, who through long years have known the ebb and flow of the Salient, who have witnessed the dissolution of its monuments into dust, and have seen its woods and pastures incredibly churned and twisted, rent and upheaved to make a diplomatic holiday; how we, who for all time will be haunted by Ypres, have hated, yet with equal passion loved, that Inferno before which the most terrifying vision of Hell becomes but a playground.

The Battles of Ypres tested the qualities of human courage, fortitude, patience and self-sacrifice, unmatched by any other struggle in all the anguish of world history. No one will ever believe, who has not ventured through the storm of steel across the muddy fastnesses of Passchendaele, where death in rat-chewed flesh and gas-bleached bones grinned from every shell-hole; or who has not wallowed through the black slime of Dumbarton Lakes, and finally has found a moment of gaseous sanctuary in the dirty depths of Tyne Cott's pillbox, that men lived and triumphed under conditions which so numbed the limbs and paralysed the spirit. "They were a wall unto us by day and night."

If we, who knew Ypres and suffered in its Salient, love Ypres, it is because the qualities of comradeship which found expression there, and the self-sacrifice which was hourly demanded, transcend all other human emotion and have consecrated for us for all time the fields and copses and bitter landscape of that area of all men's heritage. There sleep for ever tens of thousands of our comrades whose physical and spiritual experience was so uniquely attuned to our own. No one who did not know Ypres can ever realize to what depths human emotion was stirred when we lay shoulder to shoulder in a shell-hole, beneath the scourge of *trömmel feuer* under pitiless rain with death all around; or were miraculously saved to share a blanket for a few sweet hours of human confidence and communion in the bowels of the earth, foetid, rank and sticky.

Every stone, every tree of the Salient became for us haunted with memory. If the pilgrim—and he cannot be otherwise described—wanders alone along the Menin Road, up through Zonnebeke, on to the Ridge to the east, or farther north to Passchendaele, and faces west, to-day, and for so long as pilgrim veterans return to review the battlefield, in truth they must confess that here, as they survey the Salient, though they never yielded to the foe, their hearts have been surrendered to a love passing that of women.

How many cameos of that comradeship of endeavour do we not remember! From the gay lights of Poperinghe, the estaminets of Abeele, the quiet lakes of Dickebusch and Zillebeke, often lashed to fury by shell-fire, and from the battles which raged in Sanctuary Wood, Stirling Castle, even before the honeycombed ramparts of the city.

The Ypres battlefield, both in its spiritual and topographical features and formation, is, nevertheless, wholly different from the other scenes in

" THE LAST LINE OF DEFENCE "

From a drawing by Gilbert Holiday.

THE BATTLEFIELD OF YPRES

Sir D. Y. Cameron, R.A.

Flanders and near-by Picardy in which was played out the drama of the World War. Although strategically Bailleul and Hazebrouck formed the Command positions and bases for operations extending north, but especially south, beyond the immediate battlefield of Ypres, and it may be difficult to separate the fighting in 1914 on the Franco-Belgian frontier from that of Ypres itself; or, again, to detach the mighty battles of the Lys and of Mont Kemmel from the Ypres Salient, yet this triangle, with its apex at Passchendaele, preserves a distinctiveness wholly its own. It is curious, too, that the Ypres battlefield is confined within the political frontier separating Belgium from France. You step across this artificial line, but at once on the French side there is perceived a country quite different from that which is focused upon the town of Ypres. Even the inhabitants are different, for they speak Flemish, and wear a costume not unlike that of the peasants of Holland.

Although few less men gave their lives in this arena than are commemorated on the Somme, the greatest battlefield of the Western Front, there is not attached to the Salient the same sense of tragedy which everywhere pervades the Somme. The Third Battle of Ypres, from September to December, 1917, was charged with the same high hopes on the part of the Staff and an equal optimism on that of the troops who took part; the latter possessed no further illusions concerning the possibilities of a " break through," carried out in the ill-favoured conditions of autumn warfare. For them the battle

N

was another " push," a renewal of the blood bath, which by sheer weight of numbers and not less of metal hurled through the air would weaken the German resistance. " Third Ypres " was fought by fatalists, possessed of no illusions concerning its outcome, and quite certain that the odds of life and death were weighted heavily against every single individual who took part in the attack.

But although the horrors of Passchendaele and of Broodseinde and of the quagmires which lie in between, named in the heyday of their fame " Dumbarton Lakes," rival everything else on the Western Front, the associations of Ypres will be those rather of stubborn defence than of the inglorious victories which haunt the Somme. In Picardy the whole weight of the British Army was thrown against the German defence. The Memorial at Thiepval commemorates 73,357 men whose bodies lie somewhere on the fields and in the copses, and have never been found nor identified. At Ypres, a far lesser battlefield, upon the Menin Gate Memorial there are commemorated 54,896 whose fate is unknown beyond the fact that somewhere within this small triangle they disappeared and were not seen again. But Ypres differed also from the other battlefields because, although men might be shot or blown sky-high at any moment and in any sector of the Western Front, it was at Ypres alone that men could meet death by drowning.

No man of British blood can but glow with pride having the history of the defence of Ypres before his mind. Not once but three times Germany challenged this gateway of the Channel Ports, and three times British troops, immensely outnumbered, refused to surrender the city to the invaders. Throughout four years the jagged tower of the shattered Cloth Hall kept its eastern watch. The town of Ypres itself, amid whose flaming streets the Guards thrust back the legions of Germany : Gheluvelt where the thin line of Worcestershires, already almost annihilated, returned to counter-attack and rout the invading hosts : Langemarck and St. Julien, where the tiny army of seven Divisions of 1914 stood its ground before the pick of the world's greatest military force; and the entrenchments at the Hooge, where the Canadian Corps, without protection, endured the first horrors of a gas attack—these are memories with which the Ypres Salient should primarily be associated.

Yet no one who witnessed the spectacle of Third Ypres and of Passchendaele can ever quite escape its hideous impressions. If the aftermath of the Somme tortured men to the extreme limits of human endurance, the grotesque attacks of Passchendaele very nearly succeeded in destroying the morale of the finest fighting force which ever took the field. It is recorded that a high Staff Officer, visiting the battlefield near Passchendaele when it was learned that more than 100,000 casualties had been sustained without the gain of a single important objective, turned from the scene exclaiming bitterly, "And to think we asked men to fight in that ! " And Marshal Foch, who made his opposition to the venture well known, exclaimed, " Boche is bad and

boue is bad. But Boche and *boue* together . . .
ah ! " There is a wealth of significance in such a
dismissal of a project which so fascinated the minds
of the High Command that it precipitated England's
last reserves in a gamble which from the first moment
never had a chance of success.

Let us look once more at these towns and villages,
which we knew only as ruins.

Passchendaele is a village of most ancient foundation, having been known as Pascandala as early as
1055. The church, which was the scene of the
most bloody battles, was built in the eleventh century. The village was completely razed to the
ground, but the new church has been fashioned to
the model of that which previously existed.

Poperinghe, known as " Pop," where " Toc H "
was born, is a considerable town ; and though
filled with troops throughout the period of the
War, escaped serious bombardment, though both
the town itself and the surrounding villages suffered
considerably from air raids during 1918. For a
period Sir Douglas Haig had his Headquarters in the
town ; while King George V, the Prince of Wales,
Lord Kitchener, Sir John French, and Marshals
Foch and Joffre frequently reviewed troops in
the Square. At Lovie Château, close by, took place
a remarkable meeting between King George, Haig,
Foch, Joffre and Monsieur Poincaré during 1918.

It is not uninteresting to have some knowledge of
the pre-war history of those principal villages whose
names during the Great War became epic in the
story of the courage and fortitude of the human

race. In the mediæval ages every village was a
Seigneurie, and to many were attached abbeys and
monasteries which played their part in the moulding
of Flemish history. Certain names stand out.
Langemarck possessed a huge old château, known
by the name of Domanal huis ter Menneken.
Zonnebeke was formerly within the forest of Dickebusch ; and indeed the whole of this countryside was
far more thickly wooded than was the experience
of those who floundered from one copse to another.

Gheluvelt was distinguished by a noble château,
named Van den Peerboom, and in its grounds
the 2nd Worcestershires fought one of the most
notable actions of the War in 1914. The château
is depicted in a famous picture of this action ; [1] but
with the rest of the village it was levelled to the
ground by subsequent bombardments. The word
" Dickebusch " signifies a thick forest, but it is
remembered for its lake, about half a mile long,
surrounded by tree stumps. From the air Dickebusch, like Zillebeke, was always an excellent landmark ; while to men on foot the sudden appearance
of its turgid waters presented a rendezvous of
which there was no other sign than a mark on the
map. Messines, with its tremendous tactical importance, was more interesting. It possessed an
abbey established by the Princess Adele, daughter
of Robert, King of France, in 1065. Four abbesses
of royal blood of France had governed the monastery until its suppression by Republican troops in
1793. Formerly Messines enjoyed great prosperity,

[1] Now in the Officers' Mess of the 2nd Battalion.

and was a centre for the textile industry and of culture. During the war between the English and the French, of which the siege of Ypres in 1383 constituted one of the principal episodes, Messines was subjected to all the barbarity of mediæval warfare. The town was sacked and burned by the English, " *de telle manière que des deux milles maisons dont elle se composait, il n'en resta qu'une ou deux.*"

Century after century Messines re-raised its head, only to be stricken by fire, by war, by revolution; until, during the war between France and Spain in the seventeenth century, the town was reduced to the depths of misery. The great Empress Maria Theresa suppressed the abbey in 1776, but happily converted it into a house for the education of the daughters of soldiers killed or maimed in fighting for their country.

Wytschaete was also of ancient foundations. The family of Wyts came from Béthune; and in 1421, cadets of this house accompanied the Duke Philippe le Bon as an ally of the King of France against the Dauphin, later Charles VII, King of France. In the Wyts château was celebrated the marriage between Charles Temeraire and Margaret of York, the service being conducted by the Bishop of Salisbury. The village was totally destroyed during the War; but one link with the past was saved, namely the sixteenth-century clock on the church with its Flemish inscription, which has since been replaced.

Mont Kemmel, if only as an important landmark, is always interesting. The château at its foot was notable for its gardens and for a long succession of

cavalier families who ruled over the Seigneurie.
The summit and wooded slopes of Kemmel were
battered beyond belief during the German offensive
of 1918.   On the 25th April, after several days of
battle, with incredible gallantry, the Germans captured the summit[1] and overthrew the British and
two French Regiments who were holding the hill,
taking as prisoners the greater part of the defence.
No counter-attacks succeeded in dislodging the
Germans thereafter, who did not give up this prize
until the final offensive, of which its capture was
the first episode.   Mont Kemmel is over 400 feet
high, rising immediately from the plain around it.
Not far distant is the village of Locre, beneath the
Scherpenberg, a height of 300 feet similar in formation to Mont Kemmel.   Locre was also destroyed
during the 1918 offensive.   Each one of the villages
in and around the Ypres Salient possesses its
foundations in some mediæval abbey; and inevitably the culture which developed had its
source in Ypres.

The total destruction of the noble city of Ypres
was a tragedy second only to the loss of those whose
lives are commemorated on the Menin Gate and
in the cemeteries of Flanders.   The famous Cloth
Hall was surpassed in its architectural beauty and
importance by no other similar edifice.   Commenced in the year 1200, it was completed in 1230.
These vast mansions served as the meeting-place

---

[1] An excellent account, *Le Mont Kemmel*, by Captain Gustave
Goes (Reichsarchiv), translated into French, also, by Lt.-Colonel
P. Waechter, tell the complete history of Kemmel.

of the weavers, as a studio for the verification of design and as a centre for the most important industry of Flanders, which at the height of its fame knew no rival. The Huguenot families, many of them engaged in the textile industry, were centred around Ypres, and it was from great houses which still bear their names that the Huguenots fled from the Spanish Inquisition. Untold labour had gone into the production of the Cloth Hall, both its interior and exterior being rich in sculpture, architectural traceries and superb examples of mediæval tapestry. At the end of the War this Cloth Hall presented less than a skeleton of its former self, only two arches from among some fifty which faced the Place alone remaining, while the historic belfry had been reduced to a battered half of its former self, its gargoyles and carved decorations having been hurled to brick-dust or crumbled into artillery roads after immense bombardment.

The Cathedral of St. Martin, built between the thirteenth and fifteenth centuries, was likewise destroyed, its lateral chapels being especially distinguished for their rich carving. Ypres was the equal of Nuremberg. The Hôtel des Postes was the last specimen of the great houses of the thirteenth century, named Steenen, fashioned in the same style as the Cloth Hall. There were other buildings of equal importance, architecturally, artistically and historically. In 1247 Ypres held 200,000 inhabitants. There were numbers of religious orders situated in the town, centring around the most

remarkable ornament of civilization of the age.
Merchants from all Europe came to Ypres, while
Kings of France and Princes of Germany accorded
to the products of Ypres special privileges within
their states. But Ypres was always a prize to the
invader and it fell to Philip Augustus in 1213. In
the fourteenth century war, civil disturbance, pest
and flux ruined the prosperity of this capital of
West Flanders.

On the 9th of June, 1383, the town was besieged
by the English Army, but the citizens displayed so
stout a resistance that the Army was forced to
retire on the 10th August. But the siege had
ruined Ypres, and many of the industrial population
dispersed. Again and again war swept over the
city, so that it is recorded by Alexandre Farnese,
the Spanish Governor, on the 15th April, 1854, that
Ypres possessed a population of no more than 5,000
souls. The city, so close to the French frontier,
was besieged and pillaged time after time and
endured ruinous impositions. Attacked by France,
by Spain and by Austria, although its population
was reduced to the extremities of misery, the soul
of its history endured in the supremacy of its
architectural achievements.

This noble monument of civilization was first
subjected to bombardment and to fire in October
and November 1914, under the eyes of the Emperor
William II himself. The British succeeded in
holding Ypres, and the larger part of the civil
population remained in their cellars during the
winter of 1914–15, but during the spring of 1915,

in the Second Battle of Ypres, the town was subjected to a terrific bombardment, and it was completely evacuated by the civilian population; its
ruins becoming the habitation of thousands of
British infantry in reserve and of growing numbers
of artillery. During the Second Battle of Ypres
the Germans reached a position within two miles
of the town to the north, to the east and to the
south. And around Ypres swayed the great battle,
backwards and forwards, until almost the end of
the War. But Ypres had been destroyed. Scarcely
one stone remained on another. The rich carvings
had disappeared, blown to powder by artillery fire.
Ancient engravings of the city and photographs
taken during 1914 show the beauties of the city.
But Ypres is no more. The war to end war had
destroyed for ever one of the most sublime monuments to civilization the world has ever known.

It is noteworthy that to Ypres came the vanguard
of the American Army for its first exercise in the
conditions of modern warfare. The officers were
installed in a labyrinth of dug-outs constructed
beneath the ramparts which ran north and south
of the Menin Gate; and the first Divisions were
placed in the trenches which ran just to the east of
Dickebusch and La Clytte, thousands of them being
disposed in the early spring of 1918 in the fields
around the hamlet of St. Jan de Biezen.

Inevitably from Ypres one looks back upon Cassel,
across the frontier in France, where for so long
lay the Headquarters of Lord Plumer. Galignani
wrote of the road leading to Mont Cassel in 1827

that it " resembled a garden walk, intersected by orchards and groves. The country continues to present the most rich and beautiful scenery. A long avenue leads to the foot of Mount Cassel, which commands the town of the same name, and serves as a public walk. Its isolated situation in the midst of the finest plains of Flanders gives it a most picturesque appearance, and at the same time affords it a prospect, the extent and magnificence of which perhaps equals the finest in the world. From the summit the sea is seen in the distance; and even the vessels may be distinguished and counted. In the verdant plain that stretches on every side, as far as the eye can reach, are situated more than one hundred villages, besides the thirty-two following towns," which he enumerates. " Cassel, the old *Castellum Morinorum*, capital of the people called Morini, from its position naturally served as a bulwark to the ancient inhabitants of the country; on this account it has often been attacked, captured and plundered. It is celebrated in history for three memorable battles fought under its walls by three Philips of France. Philip I was defeated there in 1071 ; Philip of Valois gained a signal victory there over the Flemish, and sacked the town : and Philip, duke of Orleans, defeated the Prince of Orange there in 1677." The contrast between Galignani's impression and that of the years 1914-18 marks with appalling significance the devastation and horror produced when all the arts of science are gathered to the service of war.

CHAPTER XI

YPRES BATTLES

Plumer—The Belgian hills—Tyne Cotts—Cross-roads and insignificant landmarks—Dickebusch—Third Ypres—Memorials—A cameo
of Passion Dale.

YPRES should always be associated with the name
of Lord Plumer of Messines, who commanded the
Second Army, and for more than three years was
the warden of the Salient. That Lord Plumer's
title is associated with the brilliant victory which he
achieved on Messines Ridge—brilliant because it
attained every objective with the minimum of loss,
a tactical triumph which neither under- nor over-
estimated what could be achieved by British troops,
which contained all the elements of surprise and
was governed by a strict discretion—this does not
lessen his true title to esteemed remembrance as the
defender of the Ypres Salient. And in Lord Plumer
the troops under his command had unvarying
confidence.

The Command Headquarters of Ypres were situated at Cassel, which, although remote from the
Salient and so different from its atmosphere, figured
prominently in the Battle of the Lys, when not
only the Salient itself but the whole of the British
defences in Flanders were threatened by the onrush
of the German troops in the *Georgs-Schlacht*,
focused against Hazebrouck and culminating at
Mont Kemmel within sight of Cassel.

The view from Cassel is astonishing, and it is the
last of those four eminences which rise between the

important strategic rail-head of St. Omer, the 1914-15 Headquarters of Sir John French, and the Channel Ports. In April, 1918, the Germans fought furiously for possession of Mont Kemmel, Mont Rouge, Mont Noir, and the Scherpenberg. And from Cassel the whole panorama of the British defences, standing " with backs to the wall," could be viewed. But this was when the battlefield of Ypres had extended beyond the confines of the Salient and tremendous battles raged along the whole British front. Cassel, except for its quaint beauty and wide views and its associations with Lord Plumer, is beyond the range of Ypres. Nevertheless, it is important to refer to Cassel, because thrice in the history of Britain, British troops have marched into Ypres in defence of the Channel Ports. The line of almost insignificant hills which lies west of the Salient commands the ports, even as the even more slight Broodseinde–Passchendaele Ridge governs Ostend and Zeebrugge ; and it was the obsession to turn the German right flank, resting on Nieuport, which projected the gamble in the wastes of Passchendaele.

At this distance from the Great War it is difficult indeed for anyone to picture the appearance of the Salient in 1918, though the more solid masonry of the Belgian buildings resisted complete obliteration better than did the timber and thatched barns and less heavily constructed villages of Picardy, whose very brick-dust in the winter of 1916 disappeared in the churnings of the mud. Although other battlefields of the Western Front were pitted with shell-holes, that of the Ypres Salient was entirely pockmarked. There was nowhere one square yard which did not receive the indentation of a shell; and the British defence lines of 1918 consisted of shell-holes, linked the one with another. The stream of the Reutelbeke ceased to have any certain course beyond the compass of rising ground, and, aided by unceasing rain, poured its torrent through the shell-holes, nor was there one of these which was not sunk deep in slime.

The zone, from where now stands the Menin Gate Memorial, east towards Potijze, Zonnebeke and thence up the rise to Broodseinde, marks the true centre of the battlefield whose focus is at Tyne Cotts. The Memorial here commemorates no less than 34,957 men, representative of almost the whole of the British Army. To repicture the ghastly spectacle which the Tyne Cotts area presented to men in the winter of 1917–18 now seems almost impossible. Photographs will assist imagination, but they cannot recall the voices of the night and the stench of gas mingled with that of rotting corpses. Yet, as to-day, Tyne Cotts was a very sanctuary. On the site of the Cemetery there stood a concrete pillbox, a veritable fortress within whose walls men were safe from shell-fire, even of the heaviest calibre. Before the door, which unfortunately faced east, for this stronghold was built by German hands, were hung blankets, to shield any gleam of light from the enemy, saturated with chemicals as a defence against the poison fumes of gas. Within, into which no ray of the sun ever came, lighted by candles sticking from the necks of bottles, those responsible for the defence of the ridge of Passchendaele had their Headquarters. Of all the strange commentaries evoked by the War, the fact that the British Armies held their positions with men seems the most strange, for the Germans built a series of concrete positions such as was Tyne Cotts, and held their lines by machine guns, and seldom were men seen, while the French relied mainly on the famous field-guns, the " Seventy-fives." Tyne Cotts was to the Ypres Salient what High Wood was to the Somme battlefield. From its position a wide view to the west and to the south could be obtained. But there was nothing to break a landscape of an endless series of holes filled with water often as large as a village pond but stumps of blackened trees with splintered ends, thrusting themselves from the sea of slime. These were the landmarks which served as guides for men in the Ypres Salient.

Whereas on other battlefields one might follow such a direction as " Take the road until you come to the lone tree : turn up the communication trench by the German boot sticking from the parapet, and you will find the dug-out under the old French overcoat in the front line," at Ypres, one would note by daylight the position of a group of tree stumps, named Inverness Copse or Polygon Wood, and would flounder and slither under cover of darkness, until the lattice-work of roots underfoot and tree stumps looming against a pale star-shell would tell with certainty that the objective had been reached. And then, in similar fashion, reconsider-

ing the position of the next clump, one would go
forward, until the boot gripped again the roots of
trees. Often men would miss such objectives, and
for hours would flounder helplessly from shell-hole
to shell-hole, hoping to find the post of their objective, and often would never find it at all. Alone,
lost in a wilderness of water, overwhelmed by gusts
of shrapnel and beaten down by the sweep of
incessant machine-gun fire, at last they would be
stricken, and, beyond hope of aid, would slide into
the water and be drowned. Among the 35,000
missing at Passchendaele, thousands of names are
of those who thus disappeared. One must think of
the Ypres battlefield first, therefore, as from that
blasted, cobbled road which ran from Poperinghe,
through Vlamertinghe, past the Cloth Hall and
through the Menin Gate and then up the road to
Passchendaele, on whose bleak summit lay the
British most easterly post, farther east, in fact, than
is Ostend, though the port was never threatened.

Cross-roads and insignificant bends in lesser
lanes assumed an importance which contributed to
them names which were known throughout Flanders ;
and there were farm-houses, given English names,
which were as familiar to the British troops as is
Regent Street to the Londoner. " Dirty Bucket "
means nothing upon a Survey, nor does " Hell-fire
Corner," but for thousands the first implied rest
and the latter a cross-road to avoid like the plague,
or past which to gallop the swaying gun carriages
and limbers. What appeared immense distances
during the War are now but a comfortable walk.

It would take men half a day and all night to reach the posts of Passchendaele from Ypres, though the distance is barely five miles. When the Army moved to the assault in late September, 1917, for the Third Battle of Ypres, they struggled from their concentrations in the neighbourhood of Dickebusch, through Hooge, to the higher ground overlooking Polygon Wood to Stirling Castle. Again, the distance is but five miles, but it would take a whole day to reach the position which was so unsuitably named the " jumping-off ground," for so did mud cling to the feet that men were wearied to exhaustion even before the hour came for attack. But there was nowhere to rest in the Ypres Salient. In grave peril men might lie for a brief half-hour on the sides of the timbers which formed the two or three roads to the background of the front. And so exhausted were men that they slept while ammunition waggons thundered over the sleepers and shells tore the squelching planks ; but for the most part men could only squat, as do miners in the north country, and sleep like chickens roosting on a perch.

When extricated from these morasses, in which never for more than an hour they had slept for days and even weeks on end, they would roll along the roads which criss-crossed the area between Poperinghe and Bailleul, sleeping as they marched. It sounds incredible, but it is true. Before Third Ypres men slumbered beside the waters on the northern shores of Dickebusch Lake. How Elysian it sounds, written so. Limbers almost axle-high in

o

muck, men sweating from the smallest effort of movement, yet chilled with the cool rain-laden wind. Even at this point of concentration, at least recognizable in form, for it was rather more than a series of linked shell-holes, men could but squat and huddle while sheer fatigue freed them from consciousness. And so they slept on the eve of battle. But there were water-lilies on Dickebusch Lake, and in the moat which surrounded the eastern ramparts of the city of Ypres two swans endured every kind of attack and reared a family while the battle raged.

It may be imagined that for the Battles of the Somme and of Arras the concentration of artillery could not have been exceeded. Third Ypres witnessed the most stupendous bombardment that the world has ever known. Guns of all calibres, row after row, and rank after rank, were locked almost wheel to wheel. The British batteries poured an almost incessant stream of shells overhead. The rush of air could be felt. In titanic support of the German counter-attacks, delivered by the redoubtable Bavarians, the enemy artillery hailed ammunition upon the British support lines and communications, making each one of the slender duck tracks which led to the front a path of death, upon which platoons and isolated men danced and staggered until overwhelmed and flung into the yawning shell-holes on either side. Where ploughed fields and root crops now flourish, skeleton hands waved above gangrene waters; the stricken carcasses of mules displayed hideous entrails, making men retch at the sight; and everywhere huge sleek rats, the carrion of the Western Front, squeaked their delight over the feast of flesh. No wonder, then, that men preferred the risks of drowning alone in the darkness to movement in company upon the ordered tracks.

So tremendous was the roar of the bombardment that its sound could be clearly heard in Boulogne and even across the Channel in Kentish seaports and villages. The ground heaved and rocked. A tornado of earth clods and flying mud, splinters of timber, bricks and hot metal, whirled around. The swish and sigh of our own shells overhead was accompanied by unceasing crashes as the German shells roared a gigantic defiance. It seems unbelievable that Londoners could have captured the Broodseinde Ridge, and held it; and that the Australians wrested the sticks of Polygon Wood from the hands of those who held this figment from the map, an island in a sea of water-logged shell-holes, armed with machine-guns and with machines even more evil than those which hailed lead, the *flammenwerfer*, which showered the attack with flaming spirit.

Between the Menin Road and Houthulst Forest, which lay on the northern edge of the battlefield, separating it from the unfought swamps of north-western Belgium, with the Passchendaele Area of the Ypres Salient, its bitter apex, there are great numbers of cemeteries and memorials, each one of which marks moments pregnant with historical association in the defence of Ypres between 1914

and 1918. And the names by which many of
them are known recall for all time the familiarities
of the British Trench Map, and of names whose
significance none who served at Ypres failed to
understand. " Belgian Battery Corner," a mile to
the south of Ypres, recalls a dressing-station, with
its cottage at a cross-road, untouched and never
shelled. There is Bridge House Cemetery at Langemarck and Track X Cemetery at St. Jearrles, those
of Sanctuary Wood, and Railway Dug-Outs, Spoil
Bank, Larch Wood and Bedford House, simple,
homely names, invested with heroic glory, now
preserved in their cemeteries.

There are Memorials to the Canadians at Passchendaele, to the New Zealanders at Gravenstafel,
to the 38th Welsh Division near Boesinghe and to
the 49th Division hard by. The 7th Division, the
last of the first which took the field in 1914, is commemorated at Langemarck; and the 50th Territorial Division at " Oxford Road," a mile east of
Ypres. The Gloucestershire Regiment, which never
showed the crest worn on the back of its cap, has
its Memorial beside that of the King's Royal Rifle
Corps at Hooge. The 19th Infantry Brigade,
which in 1914 was known as French's Flying
Brigade, unattached, to be hurled into any breach
of the little Army, originally was formed from the
1st Middlesex, the Cameronians and the 93rd Highlanders, to whom were added the 5th Scottish Rifles,
one of the first Territorial Battalions in the field ;
and then re-formed with the Cameronians, the 5th
Scottish Rifles, the 2nd Royal Welch Fusiliers and

the 20th Royal Fusiliers in 1915; and re-formed again after the Battle of the Somme without the Royal Fusiliers. This Brigade formed the spearpoint of some of the greatest actions on the Western Front, as its Memorial at Zillebeke, close beside that of the 1st Battalion the South Wales Borderers, testifies.

At Polygon Wood, as well befits it, is the Memorial to the 5th Australian Division, and within this sector are some fifty cemeteries which hold the earthly remains of those known and unknown who kept the shattered tower of Ypres in its eastern watch.

Those who lie in the Ypres cemeteries number but a few more than those whose names are commemorated in the Menin Gate Memorial to the Missing. Throughout Belgium there are 92,288 buried in identified graves. But the total of dead commemorated, whose graves are not known, numbers 102,424; and these bare statistics tell the story of the Ypres Salient with greater emphasis than can words. They died somewhere in those wastes, unknown.

That every mother may yet hold her dreams to her bosom; that every wife and sweetheart may keep her love undimmed; that every son and daughter may take pride in the generation which bore them; and that those who follow after shall not forget, I contribute a cameo, a swift impression of the field of Passchendaele.

One name always struck cold horror in the heart—Passchendaele. The thunderous roar of the guns exceeded pandemonium. The boom of cannon was accompanied by the ceaseless clang of metal, blasting masonry and clattering against tree stumps. It was as if giants beat ten thousand tom-toms, while raving fanatics smote all the instruments of death in wild disharmony. The chatter of machine guns throbbed maniac melody to the peal of cannon. Always, from somewhere out of the gloom unseen voices chanted " Water ! Give me water. For Christ's sake give me water ! " And staccato voices shrieked through the night, " Hell ! . . . God ! . . . Kamerad ! . . . Mein Gott ! " . . . Cries so often silenced in a gurgle as a warrior sank beneath the soggy slime, drawing a last breath of gas, with oxygen twice laden with hydrogen. The urgent plea for water was at last fulfilled.

The dulcet notes of spinning metal and the hissing of spent bullets made known their plaintive wail, accentuated against the din of gun-fire. One sound alone for each man beat with deafening certainty—a heart knocking in a wheezing throat.

I grew to love the Passchendaele Salient. The eeriness of the bleeding landscape haunted me : seemingly endless miles of rotting life lying crazily in seemingly endless stagnant pools. Danger, deadly danger was always present, dogging the footsteps and ahead. On either side death lurked, a will-o'-the-wisp, luring the unwary to the pools from which waved skeleton fingers, beckoning. And death shrieked suddenly from on high, breathing fire and gas and molten metal, and roared his laughter in great gusts as men slithered and sank into mud, stifling laughter, mocking the vale of tears.

I recall the mood and how curious were my sensations and feelings in one great effort eastwards. . . .

I go on through the darkness. My eyes have learned to penetrate its blinding blackness. Shapes and forms appear and disappear. I heed them not. Some are tree stumps and holes, corpses and carcasses. They are still. I realize their attitude and manner.

Others move, figures like myself, hurrying, groping, stumbling, slipping. Going on. Some lurch against me if we pass. Of what use a greeting or a curse? It must be shouted to be heard, and then either becomes absurd. We go our way, deafened, yet the ear pierced always with the chant of " No-Man's-Land ": " Stretcher-bearer! give me water."

The legs carry the body mechanically; the brain knows the body's destination. On. If no metal strikes me I shall blunder on. The mind wanders. What dreariness, what boredom, even when the ground heaves suddenly before the eyes leaving a yawning hole to trap the unwary foot and drag the body, and the earth shrieks and belches above the tempest.

Time and reason—both have ceased. They are insignificant, inexplicable. Only the earth shudders, and hate justifies itself in staggering noise. Little lights soar into the air, tremulously, like children's fireworks. They do not break the blackness, illumine only themselves as with a halo. All days are the same ; all nights, but each night is for itself distinct.

The earth, the heavens, the body, the spirit closes in upon the self ; the living-dead-thing which goes on and on and on. . . . It perspires. The beads of sweat grow cold in chill wind. I am neither hot nor cold. I am nothing.

Yet last week, or perhaps five months ago—what a mockery is time in relation to the senses !—I saw the sun steal in from behind the blinds and light soft linen in a bedroom, and the darkness of night was tender and quiet. My mother crept into the room to peep at her boy as she had done when I was a little fellow. I lay on my side gazing at the familiar furnishings and pictures on the walls, whose shapes and forms I knew and could decorate and colour. And I heard the door handle turn and closed my eyes, feigning sleep, with its deep regular breathing. She held a candle, its light shielded by one hand, and looked at me, then so gently touched the hair on my brow with her lips and turned and went out. I dared not look at her bent figure, but heard her slippered feet padding quietly over the carpet. How sweet to have died then !

The candle resembled the Very light hovering above the next horizon, very faint with its own halo. My boots squelch hideously in the morass— so different from moccasins upon a deep pile. A dream—perhaps it was not true—there is no truth but I and my thoughts.

I go on . . . time is nothing . . . and space ?—
I do not know. The lights are nearer. Death
stalks closer. He no longer leaps and bounds in
wild, haphazard ecstasy. His is now a heavy, steady
tread marching across my path. I heed him not.
I go on.

I may wake to find the sun streaming past a blind.
The lights are gone, as my mother's candle was
shut out by the closed door. I close my eyes as
death stares down upon me, and I feel his breath
upon my head, a caress. But he did not kiss me.
His footsteps are going away now.

I have killed and killed again. The machine gun,
miraculously carried and mounted, spouted fire.
Black figures looming in front pitched headlong into
holes, splashing, gulping as they fell. Bombs have
been tossed at other shapeless bodies lurking and
bobbing beyond; they too have melted into the
landscape, shrieking until slime stifled sound. I
have stabbed, trodden faces and bodies more deeply
into the mud. Death has passed on to throw a
curse and gob upon new-comers, dance with them,
kiss.

My God! What weariness. No need to go on.
The brain commands a halt.

I shall sleep now. " Mother ! " someone calls.
My eyelids hang heavily and refuse to lift themselves. Who will peep at me ? I do not know. I
am tired. I must give myself to sleep. Perhaps
death will come again to seek the passion of a kiss
deferred. Who knows ? I do not care.

It is comforting in the trench bed. I gather its

clothes about me. Sacking, an abandoned over-coat, and the still warm pillow of a corpse.

The sun, a pale mockery of its bright self, seen through dust and smoke, illumines the unfamiliarity of the bed-chamber. Furnishings of bombs and ammunition boxes, for pictures the battered skulls of men, open mouths flecked with bloody foam, blind staring eyes. The light peeps from behind balks of timber, above the ledge of mud. The coverlet is grey, stained red.

No ugly dream, no nightmare this. No sudden madness. Awful ghastly sanity. " Stand to ! Action ! Front ! "

CHAPTER XII

THE LYS AND NEUVE CHAPELLE

Backs to the wall "—Neuve Église—Losses—Bailleul—Indian in defence, 1914—Messines, 1914, 1917—Ireland and New Zealand—Mont Kemmel   Flemish life.

THE battlefield of Ypres extends also some ten miles south of the city of Armentières. Apart from the notable victory at Messines, it includes also the Battle of " Plugstreet " (Ploegsteert) of October, 1914, and the epic struggle for Bailleul and Mont Kemmel in 1918, officially summarized as the Battle of the Lys. In this last, within forty-eight hours, the Germans, advancing with extraordinary skill, undaunted bravery, and almost bewildering speed, seized from the British the hard-won Messines Ridge, burst through and overwhelmed the lines held for four years at Neuve Église, Ploegsteert and Armentières, reached Bailleul, seized the city, but were held at Meteren, the very gateway to Lord Plumer's Headquarters at Cassel, the last eminence between the British Armies and the Channel Ports at Calais and Boulogne. It was at this moment of high peril to Lord Haig's vital communications that he himself penned the historic Battle Order, commanding his troops in these impressive words :

" There is no other course open to us but to fight it out. Every position must be held to the last man. There must be no retirement. With our backs to the wall and believing in the justice of our cause, each one of us must fight it to the end." No retirement was indeed possible. In front of Hazebrouck and Cassel the British Army must stand or fall. It stood.

Perhaps it would be ungrateful here to specify in any kind of detail those Battalions which especially contributed to the result, but the Battle of the Lys surging upon a territory of which Ypres is the fulcrum, was not only the turning-point of the Great War, but it secured England, it saved France it defeated the last hope of the German High Command, it reshaped the History of the World.

Although one of defence, fighting against over whelming odds, the battle was without doubt the greatest victory on the Western Front. Napoleon greatest of all military leaders, has said that in war moral is to physical as three is to one. After the Lys, defeat stared Germany in the face. After the Lys, with a unified command on the Western Front the crumbling armies of Britain and of Franc realized as never before that victory lay within their grasp, not a victorious march to Berlin as men pictured before the opening of the Somme, but one of attrition, which had broken and would finally destroy the steel front of the invader.

Outstanding perhaps was the contribution of the 33rd Division between April 11th and 18th. De nuded of a Brigade, flung into a disintegrating battle front in which a breach three miles in width had been forced between Merris and Bailleul, this one Division defied the attacks of no less than eleven German Divisions which sought to penetrate the breach. In the War Diaries of the German Fourth Army, which were captured, General Von Lossberg

Chief of Staff, in a despatch to Von Ludendorff wrote :

> Our troops encountered everywhere in the field an attack of very solid defence, well distributed in depth and particularly difficult to overcome on account of the numerous machine-gun nests.

The 33rd Battalion of the Machine Gun Corps, pivoted on the higher ground on which stood the Hoegenacker Mill, "piled the enemy dead before their guns. Nothing could dislodge them." The redoubtable German Leib-Regiment from Bavaria, after a series of victories in Roumania and Italy, records that for the first time it met opposition and was unable to advance, except for a few metres, and then only with enormous losses. The vital breach, giving access to the rail-head at Hazebrouck, within sight of Cassel, was held against attack after attack by overwhelming forces with less than 1,000 men and 32 machine guns. To the north-east of Bailleul at Neuve Église, the 2nd Worcestershires, surrounded in the church and *Mairil*, having fought a desperate action in which the chaplain greatly distinguished himself, hurling bombs from the verger's door, finally extricated themselves from the buildings and withdrew into our new line. The losses to the Division in these six days amounted to 145 officers and 3,302 men ; and on the 22nd April, Monsieur Clemenceau, "The Tiger," President of the French Republic, came personally to convey to the Division the thanks of the French Republic for their iron defence of an essential line.

History witnessed the giant blow by Germany to wrest a victory from the Allies, directed first to the overwhelming of the Fifth Army on the Somme, and then to the capture of the Channel Ports and the separation of Haig's Line of Communications from his Base in the Battle of the Lys. And it was here, held by the most dogged resistance chronicled in the annals of war, that German policy was deflected. Ludendorff released his pressure and hurled fresh Divisions against Amiens and the road to Paris with the object of separating the British from the French Army. Whether that attack had been successful or not, Clemenceau had said : " I will fight in front of Paris, I will fight in Paris, and I will fight behind Paris." But the stubborn defence of the British troops in the Battle of the Lys and by the Australians before Amiens secured the Allied cause.

Although Germany attacked along the whole front between the River Marne and the sea, and on this front the British loss totalled 14,803 officers and 288,066 men, more than one-quarter of the total number of British troops under Haig's command when the battle opened, the losses on the Lys were the heaviest in killed and wounded ; and the courage of the British Army never rose to greater heights than here. The German losses during the twenty-eight days between the 21st March and the 18th April totalled 12,807 officers and 335,962 men ; but the very flower of the Army perished before Meteren, Bailleul and on the slopes of Kemmel.

The southern section of the Ypres battlefield is

possessed of memorials which colour the history of the War from 1915 until the Armistice. The towers and spires of Bailleul, a town so familiar to British troops up till April, 1918, when the city was deserted and blasted into ruins, were the focus point for thousands of men who fought the early actions at Wytschaete, Messines, Ploegsteert and Armentières in 1914. At Wytschaete, the 3rd (Dismounted) Cavalry Division was exposed to a terrific ordeal on the 30th October, 1914, when it was assailed by masses of Infantry from the 2nd Bavarian Corps. This part of the line witnessed the most extraordinary mingling of Allied troops. To stem the attack, Indian Infantry (the 129th Regiment I.A.), from wild Baluchistan, fought shoulder to shoulder with the French Battalions who came to the succour of the cavalry and yeomanry. Wilde's Rifles, from the Punjab, fought side by side with English Infantry; while the German Emperor appeared in person on the field to encourage the two Bavarian Corps. French Zouaves from Africa filled a breach on the Menin Road beside Zillebeke.

The losses among British troops were stupendous, those, for example, of the 1st Division amounting to seventy-five per cent. of its strength, and that of the 7th Division being reduced from 12,000 Infantry to 2,333 ; while the eleven Battalions of the Second Corps by the 4th November represented only 3,500 rifles. Again and again Wytschaete was steeped in blood ; but not again to so grim a purpose as in the early winter of 1914. With the objective, as in 1918, of the Channel Ports, the *corps d'élite* of

Germany, the Guards of the German Army, were flung against the 1st Brigade, Guards facing Guards, as at Fontenoy in 1745.

The ridge of Messines, with its noble Memorials to the famous London Scottish and to the New Zealanders, preserves its fame, not only for the most brilliant British victory on the Western Front, but as a model action. The battle, which opened on the 7th June, 1917, secured nine miles of commanding country from Ploegsteert in the south to Hill 60 in the north. Hill 60, purchased for the British nation, lies just south of Wytschaete and possesses immortal memories of the old 13th and 15th Brigades. Messines especially immortalizes the contribution of India, when Indian aid in 1914 was so urgently required. In 1917 Plumer seized back into British keeping a great tract of country reddened with the mingled blood of British and of Indian soldiers.

The Messines Ridge preserves for all time the patriotic gallantry of the Irish, in whose ranks the great Irishman, Willie Redmond, fell at the head of his men. And the victory was largely gained by Australians and New Zealanders, who secured its highest point. Apart from the capture of the ridge, 7,200 prisoners were taken together with 67 guns, 294 machine guns, and 94 trench mortars, all with a loss of but 16,000 men. Directly south, on the road to Armentières, is the village of Ploegsteert, in whose woods before the winter of 1914 lulled the battleground to fitful slumber were fought out bitter hand-to-hand encounters. Grim, terrible,

THE CEMETERY AT MONT ST. ELOI

Sir H. Hughes-Stanton, R.A.

H.M. THE KING AND H.R.H. THE PRINCE OF WALES WITH GENERAL LORD RAWLINSON AND PARTY AT THE GRAVESIDE OF PRIVATE PENNINGTON, NEAR ST. GEORGE'S HILL, 10TH AUGUST, 1916

Imperial War Museum Photograph.

awe-inspiring, just west of these villages, rises the
mount of Kemmel, for possession of which Ludendorff threw Division after Division into the battle,
and in defence of which British and French troops
piled high their dead. And then, rather than pursuing the battle line farther south for the moment,
the traveller will probably follow the road back to
Bailleul.

The early days of the War witnessed migrations
on a large scale from the battle zone, for the most
part voluntary; though often, also, compulsion was
necessary. Almost up till Christmas 1914, a dogged
Flemish peasant would follow the plough behind
his horse, a white Percheron, within two hundred
yards of the British front line near Houplines.
And, as the swaying battle line settled itself to
entrenchments, the civilian community, throughout
the great area which had become the battlefield of
the Lys, continued the pursuits of peace, farming,
and with almost every other house an estaminet,
in which *vin rouge* and *vin blanc* were sold to thousands. They did a roaring trade in wine and small
groceries and postcards among the men who were
billeted in barns and houses behind the front lines.

The villages of Nieppe, Steenwerck, Laventie,
Estaires, Merville, and farther west those of West-
outre, Flêtre, Strazeele and Merris, with hundreds
of farm-houses, familiar mostly for their bowdlerized
Flemish names, bore the semblance almost of
English villages, packed with lads playing football
and marching to and from the baths and " de-
lousing stations." No plague visited on Egypt can

P

have equalled that of the lice of Flanders, wherein
to cleanse men it was necessary to erect special
stations and maintain a corps of men and Flemish
blanchisseuses to give to soldiers some respite from
this maddening irritation. At Erquinghem, millions
of lice must have suffered execution beneath a hot
iron, while to rid the kilts of these pests, hot skewers
were inserted in the pleats, upon impact with which
the fat bellies of the lice burst with an audible pop.

Merville was where the boyish figure of the
Prince of Wales first became familiar in early 1915
as a Second Lieutenant of the Grenadier Guards;
while in the surrounding villages the magnificent
physique and handsome countenances of Pathans,
Baluchies and Sikhs thronged the village streets and
houses. The peasant population became entirely
accustomed to conditions of war which caused an
endless stream of soldiers to use their houses and
their barns for billeting and their pastures in which
to tether their animals and to park limbers. Poultry
and cattle filled the yards and fields; while, apart
from the sale of eggs and vegetables, a considerable
business was done in washing for soldiers. Millions
of shirts must have passed through the wash-tubs of
Flanders.

But then, in April 1918, came swift tragedy. In
one bound the German Armies recaptured Messines,
seized Armentières, and swept over the villages
which lay east of Hazebrouck. The peasantry, who
in ignorance hurled abuses at the British troops,
everywhere filled the roads to the west with carts
and gigs, piled with such belongings as they could

snatch from burning farm-houses, and pitifully
trailed westwards from the havoc of their homes and
fields. The young corn was trampled. The roam-
ing cattle were shot down in the fields and estaminets
emptied of their liquor. And yet, it must be
recorded, scarcely had the bugles of " Cease
Fire " announced the Armistice than back came
the Belgian peasantry to take up their tasks almost
where they had been left.

This Flemish corner of Belgium will also always
be associated with the name of King Albert of the
Belgians. In defence of his invaded and battered
Kingdom, the British Armies were frequently impressed by his presence near the battlefield. Farther
north, beside Nieuport, the King had his Headquarters at La Panne in personal command of the
Belgian Army. But he visited both Locre and
Lovie Château, and often inspected British troops
as they defiled before him. The presence of the
King contributed a moral support to the defence
which it would be hard to estimate. His movements became a myth, his name a legend. He
went often alone, unrecognized in his khaki uniform ;
and it was only afterwards that those who had seen
him would learn that the tall, sombre figure ruled
over Ypres and was the sovereign master of the
Salient.

Once, it has been recorded, he passed beside a
wayside Crucifix, and before it saw two children
saying their *prières Dieu*. Their voices recited the
familiar words of the Lord's Prayer—". . . and
forgive us our trespasses,"

"As we forgive them that trespass against us," continued the King in a firm voice, a message from the King of kings to His subjects passed on by their earthly King. Almost does the Ypres battlefield and that of the Lys confine itself within the political frontiers of Belgium. But not quite, for Armentières and Bailleul lie just the other side in France. But Armentières, with its official sanction as a separate battlefield, is so filled with rich memories that it stands apart. And thus the tale of the Ypres battlefield is that of Belgium; and the history of Belgium between 1914 and 1918 is almost alone that of Ypres.

CHAPTER XIII

ARMENTIÈRES

War songs—The trench diary of an eye-witness, 1914–15—Death of an army and Neuve Chapelle.

IMMORTALIZED in a soldiers' song, often so ribald in its verses, if Armentières had no other claim to remembrance, the town gave birth to the spirit which sang in Flanders.

Standing beside the River Lys, but a mile behind the front line which endured from 1914 until April, 1918, Armentières was also the very focus of the Battle of the Lys. In one stroke the city, whose cafés, shops and houses had given shelter and hospitality to hundreds of thousands of soldiers, was eclipsed by invasion. But Armentières is primarily associated with the life of the British Army from October, 1914, until the summer of 1915. The old front line traced itself through Houplines, less than a mile east of Bois Grenier; then, with its island posts among the ditches and swamps in front of Laventie, down through Neuve Chapelle to Festubert. And within another triangle, with its apex at Hazebrouck, is the area which saw fought out the Battle of the Lys, but which witnessed also the first merging of the Old Army into the New.

When the first crude trench line, a mere ditch, was dug, the villages immediately behind the front still stood in their solid masonry. No one had even dreamed of an artillery which pulverized the villages of the Somme. Stray whiz-bangs would

bluster through the streets, scattering tiles and
shivering the glass of windows; and sometimes a
shell fired from a howitzer would gnaw a great
hole in a wall or knock the rafters all askew. But
in Armentières itself, a large part of the civilian
population continued to live far into 1915, enduring sudden storms of metal, and running to their
cellars at the first sound of alarm. The Lunatic
Asylum was a favourite billet in which a Battalion
resting from the trenches would again make itself
clean; and there were well-furnished houses with
pleasant bathrooms, whose inhabitants gave the
hospitality of hot baths, coffee and chocolate to
those relieved.

No one ever dared to define the personality of
Mademoiselle d'Armentières,[1] who gave immortality
to the song. Perhaps she was ubiquitous; or a girl
who smiled, no more, upon soldiers as they came
and went, like Suzanne, the " Peach," at the Hôtel
Sauvage in Cassel; and Marie of the Hôtel de la
Paix in Amiens. But you would find her replicas
throughout every village in this triangle at Merville,
Estaires and St. Venant.

There followed other songs, many of them, but
none which specified any other town. For this
reason, if for no other, Armentières is unique. It
can claim to have established that close bond
between the invading armies and the civilian population which, when all the irritations, the gross

---

[1] The Memorable Order of Tin Hats (MOTHS, reminiscent
of those around the Dug-out candle) of S. Africa have as their
patron Mademoiselle d'Armentières, Jean Victorine Lescornez,
selected by Monsier Briand in 1928,

discomforts, the inconveniences, the requisitions
were forgotten, was very friendly; and as the
clouds of war have blown away has mellowed into
ripe affection. This is true of the British troops,
who were foreigners to a population which had
learned little more of history than the name of
Waterloo, as it was also of the German soldiers,
who, despite the cruel necessities of war, and the
more cruel imposition of the invader, left behind
them not a little of good-will and of human charity.
Other songs sighed for home fires; and the music-
hall of London wafted to Flanders such ditties as,
"Are we downhearted? No! Never worried?
No!" Good enough for the Base camps, but a
poor measure to which to tread the mud-soaked
ways of Armentières. And "Tipperary," a few
bars of which peasant children behind the lines
would learn and shout to marching men, was
seldom sung by fighting troops. They may have
marched to it in the training camps of England, but
it was dropped overseas. A favourite, second only
to "Mademoiselle d'Armentières," was a variegated
ballad to the tune of "The Church's one foundation," which began, "We are Fred Karno's Army,"
ending with the three lines:

> Hoch! Hoch! Mein Gott!
> What a very fine lot
> Are the lads of the L.R.B. . . .

And if it was not the London Rifle Brigade on the
march then it was some other body whose name or
initials could conveniently be introduced as the
note for cynical exultation. Perhaps the heroine

of Armentières, if legend and some personal observations may be permitted to serve for authenticity, kept a vegetable and fruit store with bright green shutters in the *Place*. Be this as it may, the song is an immortal epitaph in memory of all those who chose, perhaps only to be kind, probably to be indiscreet.

Perhaps no words can more aptly describe the scenes and situations of this front during the winter 1914-15 than the bare record from a trench diary kept day by day. The first clash of arms was over. Many both in London and Berlin had imagined that the War would be swift to its finish, though not Lord Kitchener, who from the earliest moment predicted three years. The privations of the first winter campaign, without the comforts which human ingenuity and invention later devised, came as a crude shock to those who learned of them by hearsay in the warm security of homes. It seems incredible that men lived for long weeks, often waist-deep in the freezing water, with no shelter from fire or the elements beyond a layer of dripping mud overhead. But let the diary speak :

November 20th.—Bailleul. Bombs dropped on town. Billeted in long glass vineries. Thousands of pounds' worth of acres of them. Another bitterly cold night. Food very short, only bully beef.

November 21st.—Paraded 8.30 a.m. Marched to Croix du Bac. Saw Artists' Rifles, looked a good crowd. Roads very slippery—covered in ice ; large cobbles, most difficult for marching. Heavy firing on our left. Reached Armentières at 3.15 p.m. Thence to Houplines. Only 400 of the Battalion left. Freezing hard. Bivouacked in old school gymnasium. Most of roof blown off and no windows. Floor all glass and plaster.

November 22nd.—Battalion went into trenches. Remained in reserve in Bois Grenier. Billeted in house with sheets. Chucked away sheets, too cold, no windows. Bats flew into the light. Much shelling by day and heavy sniping. Farm and haystacks behind our trenches set on fire by shells : where our rations were stored.

November 23rd.—Went into trenches. Huns signalled to our snipers bulls, centres, magpies and misses. Two shells from our howitzers came overhead. Huns retaliated with shrapnel and Jack Johnsons. Very snug little mess, bit of a squash, four of us, but warm. Sounds of a gramophone in German trenches.

November 24th.—Took on dog watch 12.30 p.m.– 2.30 a.m. Desultory sniping. Took two men out to examine wire. One wounded by sniping. Finished new fire trench.

November 25th.—Very dark night. Sentries jumpy. Dog watch again. Digging all day. Our Battery behind Houplines at 11.30 a.m. fired on farm-houses opposite D Company. Effective fire. Two Allemands sent to glory. Germans retaliated by firing salvos of Jack Johnsons. Further portion of Armentières went west. At dusk went with three men to investigate farm in front of lines evacuated by Germans, brought in potatoes, entrenching tools, and a kitchen. Very dark night. Germans threw searchlights across our lines. No mail. Hideously dirty and unshaven. Dog watch again. Raining hard.

November 26th.—Hard day trenching. Rain continues. Rifles in fearful state. Bolts impossible to open, ammunition too dirty to place in rifles. Threw out sap 30 yards to left front to be operated by night if foggy so as to keep pulse of Company steady. Only three hours' rest.

November 27th.—Good news from Russia of crushing victory. Is it true? Heavy sniping. Man hit twice going to draw water at 8.30 a.m. Major R. hit in left arm. B.'s cap badge bent by bullet. Raised parapet in front. Two more men wounded. One died, hit in stomach.

November 28th.—Enemy hoisted yellow flag with black eagle in centre, we replied with Union Jack. 5 p.m. Party from A Company advanced to farm, whence snipers had been most active, and laid charge to explode it. House blown up at 7 p.m.

November 29th.—Worked hard on mess hut and roofed it in. Splendid, like a country cottage, curtained windows, 4 feet below surface of ground, with shafts leading to rear.

November 30th.—Haggis for breakfast. A large welcome mail. Bright warm day. Very quiet day. Made rum punch for the men.

December 1st.—Went to H.Q.'s at 5 a.m., and then to Armentières for a bath. Peter had found large private house. Beautifully clean and scented.

December 2nd.—One man hit in head. The King in Bailleul. Eight men went to represent the

Regiment. Mother and Baby in action. Adopted the T-trench idea. Headquarters shelled, four casualties—work of spies ?

December 3rd.—Headquarters shelled again. Five civilians killed. All our billets changed. Three of our Farman biplanes came over. Mostly boldly handled. Directing artillery fire. One casualty, man killed, shot through loophole in mouth. Peter's great jam pudding made and eaten. Very good.

December 4th.—Heavy shelling and heavy rain. Collapsing dug-outs and falling traverses. Trenches deep in water and slime. Our utensils now have names—" Bertie," the bread-knife ; " Oliver," the opener ; " Thomas," the tea-strainer, and " Horace Rumbold,"—he is Falstaffian like his name—the rum-jar ; " Martha," the milk-bottle. L. has become " Count Slabonga," and I the " Super-Man " (I know not why) ; B. continues to smoke hundreds of cigarettes.

December 5th.—Furious sniping all day, and machine gun used against our trenches, probably because Germans aware that many of parapets no longer bullet-proof. Swept away by heavy rains. Turned on Maxim guns at nightfall and searched from 300 to 2,000 yards. Cries heard from German trenches, then a searchlight switched on. Pooped at it. It vanished. First watch.

December 6th.—Poured with rain all day. Trenches diabolically wet. Peter carried a door from Bois Grenier and made me a new bivvy. At 11 a.m. A Company reported that three Germans had waved white flag from a farm in front. A sergeant went to investigate and brought them in, self-surrendered prisoners. Men of 139th Regiment, XIXth Saxon Corps. Fed up. Report much artillery mobilized on our front. Trenches more strongly held than our own. Only one meal per diem. 8.30 p.m., vigorous firing opened on our lines. Dashed out in pitch darkness up the trenches. Great difficulty in getting men into firing position owing to one platoon working on entrenchments in rear coming in without arms. Rifle flashes coming from 50 yards in front. Four of our men killed. After twenty minutes, Germans heavily shelled our position. Seven more men killed. Got hit in hand, much blood and big bruise. Many rifles jammed with dirty ammunition. (Platoon Sergeants should have spare rifles in reserve clean for use.) Carefully delivered fire by volleys of greater value than individual rapid fire. Corporal P. controlled his section well. Sergeant L. useless, an absolute panic-monger. Middle watch, 2 a.m.–3.30 a.m. Germans seen removing dead or wounded on a stretcher. A half-hearted attack. One of our advanced posts was run over and passed. German officer seen passing orders down the line.

December 7th.—Trenches taken over at 5.30 p.m., in a deluge of rain, pitch darkness, and hideous slime.

December 12th.—Walked our weary and cramped limbs to billets, the Lunatic Asylum, Armentières again. Very comfortable with a spring bed. Town in tense darkness.

December 13th.—Marched the Company to Er-

quinghem for a wash in the converted dye-works
Best-organized thing I have seen yet. Men stripped
naked, their clothes in small batches being placed in
trolleys and rushed outside where an army of
blanchisseuses with irons and fumigating liquid iron
them out. While this operation was in progress,
the men passed into another room where there
were vast vats of steaming water, and here they
washed. On returning found their clothes ready,
fumigated, washed and dried by pressure. In afternoon, went with Peter to No. 6. I had a bath and
my shoes mended. Lovely long sleep.

December 14*th*–20*th*.—In Armentières . . . attended service. Good address by Padre. Peace in
war, if the soul has peace. Our billets shelled
during church. Three men hit. B Company wall
pierced. Several men bruised by bricks and flying bedsteads. Paraded for trenches 4 p.m. Took
over worst trenches on earth. Poured with rain.
Slimy and damnable: a wicked night and bitterly
cold.

December 21*st*.—Xmas gifts pour in from all round
the countryside. My dug-out is a quagmire.
Bailed for hours, men wonderfully cheerful. Peter
keeps me amused with imaginative castles in the
air for the future—after the War. Our policy would
seem to be to hem in Germany with a wall of steel;
while our fleet makes it possible to land troops in
Northern Germany, or strengthen the combined
Serbian and Russian Armies in South-Eastern
Galicia and Austria; paralyse Austria and make her
surrender and so close the neutral Italian door into

Germany, and exhaust her. This would be costly. We can afford it. Every day to Germany means an undermined morale and a doubting population, while every day to us means an increasing army— British, French, Russians—while Japan is now freed after the fall of Tsingtau to assist us with her army. Quiet day.

December 22nd.—Snowing. A good deal of " wind " in the line. Much firing, then sounds of cheering. Bitter argument with S. and M. All very rude to each other—pacified.

December 23rd.—Great excitement in mail. Gifts to officers from Queen Alexandra. A lovely pair of gauntlet gloves, a pipe and chocolate. I received mufflers from Oxshott friends for distribution in the Company. More snow.

December 24th.—German band in the trenches. We sang in turns—Germans and ourselves. Sergeant M. exchanged badges with a German officer. Much shouting. On the *qui vive* all night.

December 25th.—Heavy frost and thick mist. Every man received a Christmas card from H.M. the King and H.M. the Queen, bearing the message " With our best wishes for Christmas 1914. May God protect you and bring you safe home. Mary R. George R.I." A great rum issue. Many expressions of good-will. In the afternoon war ceased and we advanced across our trenches and chatted with the Germans. Most amusing. Can this be war ? Some had played football against Glasgow Celtic. All were certain of a victory in about six months, for Germany, and the end of the War. They gave us cigars and cap badges. They were men of the 113th and 139 Regiments of the XIXth Saxon Corps. We parted saying, " To-morrow it is war." Mother sent me a hot-water bottle. Everyone very jealous.

December 26th.—Good deal of artillery fire in the morning. In the evening the whole Brigade relieved. Marched to the billets in the Science College. B., C., the doctor and I were in a very comfortable house, that of Monsieur Johnson. Piano, lovely beds, spacious rooms, tasteful decoration, and not much damaged.

December 27th.—Played football for the Company. Awfully sloppy ground, but good game. Long route march to Ponte de Nieppe and Erquinghem—everyone footsore.

December 28th–January 2nd.—Armentières billets.

January 2nd.—Took over trenches at Bois Grenier from Shropshires. Ghastly night and wicked trenches. The whole place a river. No sleep.

January 3rd.—Waded to H.Q's. up to my waist. Bailed all day without avail. Water gained 2 feet. No sleep. Rained all day.

January 4th.—Poured all day. Another attempt to make trench habitable. No use. Rained all day.

January 5th.—Rained all day. Worked on communication trench.

January 6th, 7th, 8th, 9th.—Life in these days too hideous to write. Continuous rain and disappointment. Bitterly cold. Numerous casualties from shell- and rifle-fire. Many sick.

January 10th.—Impossible to cook anything.

Mud, rain, sickness. Trenches washed away. Line heavily shelled with several direct hits. Difficult to assist wounded owing to heavy sniping. The smell has become awful. Have abandoned my kilt and wear it as a cape. Peter went out at night and brought back a biscuit tin of hot tea. God bless his soul!

January 11*th*.—Relieved. Bathed and cleaned off all my body lice, some as large as small scorpions. Have a bad cold.

January 12*th*.—K. and M. gone sick. L. home for good. B. sick also. Took over trenches by night at La Hussoie. Awful snow by day. Trenches practically don't exist.

January 13*th*.—Bitterly cold night. Freezing hard. Working party 9 p.m.–1 a.m. High cutting wind made it almost too cold to work. R.E. sent no material worth having. Awful night. Very wet and freezing. Rubbed each other's feet with oil. Could not lie down. Huddled ourselves in a blanket and prayed for morning. Most of B Company sick and getting frost-bitten.

January 14*th*.—Vigorous sniping. Four men badly hit on working party. Wickedly cold. Tried to sleep on a board laid over a *minnenwerfer* hole. Kept each other warm and hugged the hot-water bottle—miraculously filled. A bit feverish.

January 15*th*.—Feel pretty rotten. Visited the Company squatting under odd bits of corrugated iron and in miserable earthworks. Not connected anywhere. Had to run like hell. Heavy sniping. Legs and feet getting cramped with wet. Rub each other for half an hour every few hours. God bless tobacco, although its quality has gone to the devil! No sleep.

January 16*th.*—Started building a breastwork with hen-coop dug-outs. Germans doing the same thing. No sniping. Slept in a new hen-coop. Just room for two. Like being in a packing-case. High above the ground in view of Germans. Very quiet night, no shooting. Glorious sleep.

January 17*th.*—Bright sunshine. Stood to at 7 a.m. Allemands all running about in the open. We did the same thing and started on the breast-work. No shooting. A sort of unwritten armistice. Each minding his own business. Fires and braziers going everywhere with clouds of smoke on both sides of the line, and everyone walking about. H. visited us from H.Q. and was very rude about the fires. Had my letters home stopped for three weeks as a punishment, or must be censored by himself. Relieved at 5.30 p.m., and back to a new billet at L'Armée. Bed on flour-bags in the *boulangerie*. Beautifully warm. Perfect peace and quietness, and H. has gone on leave. We're enjoying ourselves : and Madame Caniot believes herself our mother.

January 29*th.*—Furious fighting proceeding all along the line except here. Between the Armentières Rue de Bois railway line and Burnt Farm—the sector occupied by the right wing of 16th Brigade (the Buffs) and D Company of the 93rd—owing to the fact that the water has reached the level of the tops of the parapets of both the German and our own trenches, and snow is beginning to fall, we

Q

are sitting on the parapets looking at each other while heavy sniping continues on either flank. There is no crossfire.

January 30th.—At dawn we commenced work on a new breastwork line. Large working parties approach both our own and the German lines carrying engineer material and timber. The Saxons opposite the Buffs are sharing a heavy iron-headed hammer which is thrown across the barbed wire. Two imitation Buckingham Palace Guards with fixed bayonets have been mounted, one British, one German, some 20 yards distant from each other. Special vigilance is now maintained by us. The distance of the German line from our breastwork is 60 yards across a field of turnip-tops. We converse with the Germans, who have invited us to play a football match in No-Man's-Land. Our work seems to proceed more rapidly than that of the enemy, but to be less solid. The enemy is using much cement.

January 31st.—After a gingering from the General Staff the Buffs " declared war " at 11 a.m. An " ultimatum " sent at 10 a.m. This does not seem to affect our friends. We continued building while the Buffs and Saxons tried to smash each other's work.

February 2nd.—Artillery seems by mutual agreement to have " declared war " for us. The whole of the new work on both sides is now flying in the air under high explosive.

There are twelve cemeteries east of Armentières,

whose line exactly follows the old front line. At their centre stands Ration Farm Military Cemetery. To these deserted farm-houses as dusk fell every day, men soaked above the knees in mud would come, hoping to retrieve their limbers, food for their platoons, huddled in the water between mud walls. Ration Farm was a Battalion Headquarters, an Aid Post, and on its northern side was the cemetery. Each one of these twelve occupies the same position as that upon which it was first established. Perhaps no picture provides a better impression of the type of men who endured this first winter than the Biography of a Batman.[1] It is equally an epitaph to many of those who lie in the cemeteries between Armentières and Fleurbaix, for they commemorate soldiers of the old Regular Army.

Armentières witnessed the death of an Army. For after the winter of 1914–15, Territorials, Special Reservists and the First Hundred Thousand of Kitchener's Army began to take the field. The Old Army was broken up. Most of those who had not perished at Mons and Le Cateau and had survived the winter were taken to instruct and to lead the new Armies in the field; and the face of the former Brigades was changed.

A little farther south lies the battlefield of Neuve Chapelle, the first battle in which British troops took the offensive, when ambition fired Sir John French to break the stalemate of the Western Front and to throw back the invader. The attack was

[1] *Footslogger* (Chap. X), by Lt.-Col. G. S. Hutchison.

planned with elaborate secrecy ; and the blow fell
upon an unsuspecting enemy, the trenches being
held by troops from the Seventh German Corps,
reinforced by Saxons and Bavarians. It was preceded by a bombardment of short duration, when
suddenly the guns ceased. The officers blew their
whistles ; and upon a front of 1,000 yards the troops
rose from their trenches and stormed across No-
Man's-Land. The honours of Neuve Chapelle must
be awarded to the Indian troops.

CHAPTER XIV

ARRAS AND CAMBRAI

History—Tactical importance—The Hindenburg Line—Croisilles—
The city of Arras—Losses—The Battle of the Tanks.

ARRAS, formerly the capital of Artois, and now of
the *Department* of the *Pas de Calais*, can be regarded
as the Nuremberg of the north of France, as was
Ypres that of Belgium. The very curious old
houses, arcades and sculptural glories were similar
in each of these mediæval cities.

The wonders of Ypres were powdered: those of
Arras suffered almost the same fate. Already in the
fourth century Arras was celebrated for its tapestries
and woollen stuffs, the finest examples of the former
being those in the Cathedral of Beauvais and in the
Seraglio at Constantinople. Known as Nemetacum,
Arras was the capital of the tribe of the Atrebates,
to whom a Greek priest, known as Diogenes,
preached the gospel in the fourth century and was
martyred for his pains. A former magnificent
Cathedral of the twelfth and thirteenth centuries
was sold during the French Revolution; and the
ghost of Robespierre, who was a native of the city,
must have been overjoyed when the Cathedral was
pulled down under the Empire and the Restoration.

Arras was rich in architectural wonder, the *Grande
Place*, with its market at the centre, being one of the
most picturesque in the world. But Arras was
bombarded day and night during the Great War,
being but four miles from the front lines, and the
city even connected thereto by communication

trenches and subterranean galleries. The Allied line formed a salient at this point, the trench system curling round the city; while the great Battle of Arras in April, 1917, increased the salient astride the Rivers Scarpe, the Sensée, and the Cojeul. The German Switch Line which ran through Bullecourt, Fontaines les Croisilles and thence along to Vimy was the objective of the attack.

Like the Flers Line through High Wood on the Somme, the postion commanded extensive views to east and to west; and it presented an obstacle of apparently impregnable strength, its front deeply and heavily wired, the traversed lines being set with cement blockhouses as machine-gun posts, carefully sited to rake every approach with enfilade fire. Both the front and the support lines were connected the one with another by immense underground galleries, fitted with electric light and capable of holding thousands of men.

The battlefield of Arras, which truly lies between the Bapaume–Cambrai Road and Vimy, centres at Croisilles; and it was in the struggle which ensued for the high ground on either side of the Sensée River that the fiercest fighting took place in 1917. But these undulating fields played their part also on the left of the First Battle of the Somme; and were covered by the successful drive of the Third and Fourth British Armies between the 21st and the 31st August, 1918. In the narrow sector immediately east of Arras, in what is officially known as the Second Battle of Arras, between the 26th August and the 1st September, the same

Armies in the same year captured 8,850 prisoners and 200 guns.

The heights of Bullecourt outflank Bapaume; and it was in order to make way for a further attempt to capture Cambrai that the fortunes of the British Army were tested before Arras; but it was also planned to draw part of the German Army from before the French experiment on the Chemin des Dames. A project in the war of attrition as was the Battle of Arras, the gains were achieved without the appalling sacrifices which characterized the Somme: 13,000 prisoners and 200 guns were taken. The earlier stage of the attack was attended by success; and Haig had intended to limit his objective to Monchy le Preux. But, with the French Army tottering under the failure of Neville's experiment, Haig was obliged to continue the pressure at very high cost. The aftermath of Arras is, therefore, wreathed by deep tragedy.

If you follow, on foot, the ridge which lies between Bullecourt to where it dips suddenly to the Sensée Valley beside Fontaines les Croisilles, you cannot fail to be impressed by the strength of the position. Some of the ground near Croisilles has been so mauled by entrenchments and heavy shelling that even after twenty years it remains exactly as it was. The subsoil of chalk was upheaved; and great pitfalls, clustered by white boulders, heaped with barbed wire and rusting metal, show clearly where the fiercest struggles took place. Each bank, and hedge, and ditch—and they are few as they existed—

implied a feature of immense tactical importance to the attack and the defence.

A few hundred yards to the east of Croisilles is a chalk quarry ; and into this, under cover of darkness, within two hundreds yards of the German line, on the 23rd April, 1917, were driven dozens of limbers, stacked with ammunition. The mules' feet and the wheels of the waggons were wrapped in sacks that they should not ring upon the road, while the trench mortars in the line had instructions to keep up a continuous bombardment in order to cover the sound. The operation was so successful that not a mule and not a man were lost. It is interesting to examine an air photograph of the Hindenburg Line, with its defences before the attack, and to compare this with one taken after the trenches had been subjected to enormous bombardments. " All hope abandon, ye who enter here ! " was the legend written below such a photograph attached to the map of an Infantry Officer before assaulting ground which resembled the waves of a rough sea suddenly congealed, and above them endless strands of barbed wire, some as thick as a ship's cable, the whole wreathed in a dust of smoke.

Men had learned something of war before the date of the First Battle of Arras. The new Armies of Loos were no longer untried. The infantry of the Somme had learned to face machine-gun fire and knew its penalties. No great hopes buoyed those who fought the battle. They had become part of a machine, growing always bigger and bigger, making always more noise, one in which they were less than mere cogs, and only tiny particles which, like metal dust, would be flaked off and lost in the whirr of the machine. You find their Memorials in the Faubourg d'Amiens, in Arras, to the missing; and at Monchy to the 12th Division, to the 37th and to the men of Newfoundland. The triangle with its apex on Arras is small enough, its base a little more than ten miles long, but within this area there are more than sixty Cemeteries; while in the region behind at places which marked the dressing-stations and advanced hospitals there are more than forty Cemeteries, containing the bodies of thousands of known men. The Memorial to the Missing at Arras commemorates 35,925 men; but this number is but half those whose graves are unknown commemorated in the Somme Memorial at Thiepval.

The city of Arras is at the very centre of the British battle line. When, in August, 1918, the Allied Drive to the east began, the pincers were applied at Arras and at Ypres. There was no fighting in the valley of the Lys, around Lille, Lens and Douai. The German Armies withdrew. But Arras marked the left flank of the great battles which proceeded in a series of bounds between August and the Armistice, to Cambrai, to the River Selle and Le Cateau and thence to Maubeuge. The brunt of these attacks fell on the British Army, whose captures between August and November, 1918, included 188,700 prisoners and 2,840 guns. Yet, the first task was to regain the ground captured in 1917 and lost in March, 1918.

Arras, during the later war period, changed very little. The German line was but 1,700 yards east of the market-place, but the suburbs and outlying buildings extended into the French systems. Prior to the first battle, experience had shown that every street was accurately ranged by the German artillery; and that in consequence it would prove suicidal for any attempt to debouch from the streets to be made. During the winter preceding the spring of 1917, cellars and other subterranean excavations which honeycombed the city were linked up, while fresh tunnels were also constructed. More than three Divisions came, therefore, to be secreted underground, with provision for every kind of military necesssity, including electric light, water and a light railway system. A dressing-station with seven hundred beds was also constructed. Preparatory to the battle, nearly the whole of the 7th Corps was placed in these galleries. But Arras itself was destroyed. Fine reconstructed villages mark the site of those which British troops knew only as ruins and brick-dust. Yet their plan is much as it was.

From the cemetery in Croisilles, in whose family vaults, among the leaded coffins, men took refuge from shell-fire, you can perceive the village of Fontaine, just as the British Armies viewed it before the colossal bombardment reduced the houses to dust and the trees to matchwood. Fontaine was a vital point in the Hindenburg Line, for here the high defences dipped suddenly to cross the Sensée River. It is not difficult to imagine how attack following attack up the valley was decimated by machine-gun fire from concrete posts set on the low hills which stand north and south of the village. When it is remembered that the barbed-wire entanglements built in front of the Hindenburg Line were in some cases one hundred yards thick, and the defences behind of extraordinary strength, it is of the highest credit to the valour and determination of British Armies that the high ground along the whole of the front, considered impregnable, was captured ; and the victory included 14,000 prisoners and 180 guns. But the British losses were enormous.

The losses in the operations between April and July, 1917, which included Arras, the Chemin des Dames and the comparatively far less costly assault at Messines, amounted to 355,928 of British, 279,000 French and 414,077 Germans, killed, wounded, missing and prisoners, more than 1,000,000 within four months. Within an equal period the Battle of the Somme cost more than 1,330,000 men. But as the war machine improved and engulfed more men into its process, the losses in 1918 were to go higher yet. During the period March to June, 1918, British, French and German warriors suffered 1,539,715 casualties. And the offensive campaign from July to November, 1918, totalled 1,728,369. In this last year the German losses totalled 1,498,000 men.

No story of Arras can omit special emphasis of the First Battle of Cambrai, which will rank as one of the most remarkable battles ever fought. On November 20th, 1917, from a base of some 13,000 yards in width, a penetration of no less than 10,000

yards was effected in twelve hours, 8,000 prisoners
and 100 guns were captured, and these prisoners
alone were nearly double the casualties suffered by
the Third and Fourth Armies during the first day
of battle. The attacking infantry were assisted by
a new army, a new body of men, the Tank Corps
with a strength in officers and men of a little over
4,000. The First Battle of Cambrai ushered in the
military epoch of the mechanical engineer.

> The First Battle of Cambrai was to be a single-minded
> battle. It was to fulfil in the simplest way the prime
> function of war, that is, to destroy the forces of the
> enemy.
> To attain this end it was to rely upon surprise, audacity
> and rapidity of movement.
> Its main action was to be completed in about twenty-
> four hours, during which time it was proposed to penetrate
> the Hindenburg Line, which here consisted of four
> systems of trenches.[1]

The German trenches were about sixteen feet
wide and eighteen feet deep, a gap too wide to be
crossed by Tanks without some means of bridging
the intervening obstacle. Human ingenuity devised
a fascine, constructed of stout bundles of brush-
wood, and these were fitted to the front of the Tanks
with a releasing gear operating from within, so that
when the Tank arrived before the trench, it would
automatically drop its own bridge and go over it.
Each bundle weighed one ton and a half, and it
took twenty Chinese coolies employed at the work-
shops to move one. Elaborate secrecy and a system
of planned perjury made it certain that there would

[1] *The Tank Corps*, by Williams-Ellis, p. 101.

be no leakage of information, and this was secured up till two days prior to the attack ; and it was only then that General von Marwitz, commanding the German front, had his suspicions aroused, but too late. In planning the attack, every movement and formation was reduced to an exact drill, several special exercises being evolved for the occasion. One of them, a simple platoon drill for the infantry, was, for example, based upon a drill described by Xenophon in the *Cyropædia*, and attributed by him to Cyrus of Persia, about the year 500 B.C. A further unique feature of the battle was that the attack was preceded by no preliminary bombardment, while General Elles, commanding the Tank Corps, personally led his land fleet under his flag, in the " Hilda."

The authentic Order read as follows :—

Special Order, No 6.

1. To-morrow the Tank Corps will have the chance for which it has been waiting for many months, to operate on good going in the van of the battle.
2. All that hard work and ingenuity can achieve has been done in the way of preparation.
3. It remains for unit commanders and for tank crews to complete the work by judgment and pluck in the battle itself.
4. In the light of past experience I leave the good name of the Corps with great confidence in your hands.
5. I propose leading the attack of the Centre Division.

November 19, 1917.

(Signed) HUGH ELLES,
B.-G. Commanding Tank Corps.

At 6 o'clock on the morning of the 20th, under

cover of mist, 350 Tanks moved forward, led by the
Flag Tank at its centre. Lateau Wood, Rumilly,
Masnières, Flesquières, Graincourt, Havrincourt
and Bourlon Wood marked the scene of the battle,
which was planned with strictly limited objectives. November 30th witnessed, however, a swift
counter-stroke by the enemy. The effect of the
battle had been to produce a considerable salient
extending from the British lines. General von
Marwitz, with an ambitious scheme in mind,
intended to pinch off the salient and to capture the
entire 3rd and 4th Corps which held it.

The Tank Corps had completed their work, and
were wearied to exhaustion. Nevertheless, to assist
the infantry, especially at Villers Guislain, Marcoing
and La Vacquerie, the Tanks were hastily flung
again into the battle, and terrific fighting followed.
There is no doubt that the surprise attack of the
Tanks created considerable alarm among the Germans, as is evidenced by the large number of
prisoners taken. Nevertheless, although overwhelmed by this new death-dealing monstrosity of
war, pockets of the enemy held out with desperate
courage, and Sir Douglas Haig's despatch on the
battle records :

> Many of the hits upon our tanks at Flesquières were
> obtained by a German artillery officer who, remaining
> alone at his battery, served a field gun single-handed until
> killed at his gun. The great bravery of this officer aroused
> the admiration of all ranks.

CHAPTER XV

LA BASSEE AND BÉTHUNE

Coal-fields—Béthune and St. Pol—" The Brickstacks "—Birth of
Kitchener's Army—Fosse Eight—The Prince of Wales—The Three
Graces.

THE coal-fields of the manufacturing centre of Lille
are another battlefield, distinct from those of Ypres
and Armentières to the north, and Arras to the
south.

The country is uninviting, a low-lying agricultural
district from which tower smoking chimney-stacks
and immense slag-heaps. Everywhere the grime of
coal-dust blackens the fields. The front of the
battle-line lay between the La Bassée Canal and the
Vimy Ridge. Actions of great importance were
fought within this zone, notably those of La Bassée,
1914 ; Loos, September, 1915 ; and the noble capture of Vimy Ridge by the Canadian corps under
Sir Julian Byng, ennobled as Lord Byng of Vimy,
on the left flank of the Battle of Arras in April,
1917.

This unprepossessing area is, however, distinguished by the fact that it was the scene of the
baptism of fire for the New Armies fashioned by
Lord Kitchener. It was something more than a
battlefield : it was a playground. The scattered
villages and miners' cottages served to introduce the
New Armies to that glorious life of comradeship to
whose spell the whole British Army succumbed.

Leave of absence from France to England came
once in six months, and often not once within a

year ; while in the French conscript armies a far
higher number of men were always absent from the
battle line. It must not be forgotten that of the
millions who saw service in the British Armies overseas, not more than a handful were accustomed to
being torn from the bosom of the family and from
the ways of peace, as was the familiar experience
of the conscript armies of Europe. Human nature
demands its reciprocities. This area witnessed the
foundation of an entirely new relationship between
man and man, exiled from his own home-land.

The battlefield is focused on the town of Béthune,
forming the apex of the triangle, and it is also distinguished by the fact that during 1915 it was the
area devoted to experimentation with the new
artifices of war, machine guns, trench mortars,
bombs and grenades. Béthune was to this sector
what Amiens was to the Somme, Poperinghe to
Ypres and Bailleul and Cassel to Armentières and
the Lys. But no town was ever quite like the
Béthune of 1915. From the armies had faded the
soldiers of tradition, and those who remained were
absorbed and lost in the great expansion of Kitchener's Army.

To most of those who played in Béthune the
bitterness of the Mons Retreat was unknown, the
gall of winter trenches untasted, the shock of battle
untried ; and here was the flower of English youth
and Scottish youth, Welsh and Irish too.

The New Armies took the field. They came in
easy stages, billeted on the line of march in every
village and farm-house—Lillers, Gonehem, Hinges,

ADANAC MILITARY CEMETERY AT MIRAUMONT AND PYS, FRANCE

Imperial War Graves Commission.

THE MEMORIAL AT THE MENIN GATE

The Times.

Chocques, Nœux les Mines, Hersin, to name but a few. Behind lay St. Pol, an important railway centre, hard by the battlefield of Azincourt. The fields and trees of Artois were tinted with the first green freshness of spring and early summer, upon which the chimneys no longer poured their shroud of carbon. This life of light marching and of snug barns was a novel holiday. Here was experience filled with delight, the fun of shopping in a foreign tongue, however trivial the purchases ; of courting with a kind of " dumb crambo " ; and of watching customs so alien from our own.

The trench line at Béthune was possessed of a highly organized defence system of several lines with ample communication trenches. The British and German lines lay very close to one another, with ever-present possibilities for breaking the quiet by a swift raid across No-Man's-Land. Of all points on this front the most famous were " The Brick-stacks," just east of the village of Cuinchy, and the " Hohenzollern Redoubt " a mile or so farther south. No one who did not see them can imagine the elaborate fortifications of " The Brickstacks," nor the extraordinary zeal with which mining and countermining were accomplished. During early 1915 no less than fifteen great mines were exploded beside the La Bassée Canal. The stacks were held partly by ourselves and partly by the enemy ; and the struggle which ensued was for possession of the lips of the craters formed by mine explosions. Immense as were the cavities created, they were childish compared with the mine at La Boisselle on

R

the Somme, which measured 340 yards in circum-
ference.

La Bassée witnessed the great battle between
October 12th and November 11th, 1914, lasting a
clear month. At Waterloo the losses had been
under 10,000 ; in this fight at La Bassée they were
little short of 50,000. The Germans made immense
efforts at this point, and were met first by French
and then by British and Indian troops. At Givenchy, a little farther south, the Indians, men from the
State of Bhopal, Pathans, Gurkhas, Jats and Pun-
jabis, were again submitted to a fearful ordeal.
Day after day they stood up to their knees in ice-
cold water, while the Germans attacked again and
again.

There followed that strange Christmas Armistice,
with its amazing spectacle of fraternization, where
the enemies of yesterday conversed in No-Man's-
Land, and even played games, renewing hostilities
on the following day. And early in January the
Germans again and again attacked the Guards
Division at La Bassée, hand-to-hand fighting taking
place in the brick and chalk fortifications between the
Canal and the trenches in front of Givenchy. During
the following spring, experts of all kinds came up
" Piccadilly," worked along " Old Boots Trench,"
kicked up hell in " The Brickstacks," practising all
kinds of devilry. And having practised they returned to Béthune.

The long *pavé* road leading through Beuvry,
Cambrin and Cuinchy to La Bassée, across the
German lines, was often under shell-fire. A shell

would burst in a platoon as at night new troops made their first excursion to the line. Death looked them in the eyes for the first time, curiously, grotesquely, horribly. Lads, who but a moment earlier had been jesting of some puerile adventure at Béthune, lay at the roadside, limp-limbed, torn and bleeding, breath coming in short stertorous gasps, eyes already glazed by the hand of death. On the morrow their mortal remains would be buried in the cemetery beside the rickety church in Cambrin, while the Padre intoned the burial service and scattered the dust. But this was before the era of mass slaughter, when burial rites were beyond human possibility.

In Beuvry and at Cambrin these cemeteries remain; and there was in Beuvry a well-known shop, kept by a Madame Quevy, a centre for every kind of comfort; and near Annequin, whose immense slag heap provided sooty shelter for thousands of men and its summit a superb observation post, stood the famous chemist's shop, with a most evil reputation for spies. The main street of Cuinchy was known as " Harley Street "; and close behind the front line was a large double-storied house, the eastern side of its roof painted with a great red cross, known as " No. 1 Harley Street," and never shelled, beside it the Woburn Abbey Cemetery. The Memorial to the Indian Army, none more dignified, stands at " Windy Corner " at Cuinchy; and there is another of equal architectural simplicity near Neuve Chapelle.

The streets of Béthune often saw the Prince of

Wales, heir to the throne of the mightiest of Empires, in little cafés and in tiny, homely shops. Béthune possessed a magnificent belfry, dating from 1388 ; and there were ancient houses of the fifteenth and sixteenth centuries, including that of the Grand Place, occupied by the Hôtel du Nord. Alas, these were blown to brick-dust, as was the " Lion d'Or," a famous meeting-place.

Long before the War, *La Compagnie des Mines de Béthune* had developed large coal-mines, the seams of which had been opened on both sides of what became " No-Man's-Land," south of the La Bassée Canal. The mines were over sixty years old, and production had risen from four thousand tons in 1853 to well over two million tons in 1914. The flat plains were broken and the horizon traversed by the winding gear staged above the shafts, and by twelve pitheads, at the bottom of whose shafts the seams were connected, covering several square miles of workings. The slag-heaps, known by the name of " *fosse*," numbered nine which were important ; and though in days of peace the " *fosses* " had only been excrescences of waste, in war they assumed considerable importance. " Fosse Eight," famous for the struggles which took place on its grimy sides in the Battle of Loos, lay close behind the German line ; but it is difficult to imagine that the tumbling church of Cambrin had been famous as an example of fifteenth-century architecture, containing a beautiful font of the period. Early in 1915 Beuvry Church became a dressing-station, and on its pews were laid out the wounded ; while down the aisles moved the processions of stretcher-bearers.

> Back from the line one night in June,
> I gave a dinner at Béthune——

wrote Robert Graves ; and he continued :

> Seven courses, the most gorgeous meal
> Money could buy or batman steal.
> Five hungry lads welcomed the fish
> With shouts that nearly cracked the dish ;
> Asparagus came with tender tops,
> Strawberries in cream, and mutton-chops,
> Said Jenkins, as my hand he shook,
> " They'll put this in the history book."
> We bawled Church anthems *in choro*
> Of Bethlehem and Hermon snow,
> With drinking songs, a mighty sound
> To help the good red Pommard round.
> Stories and laughter interspersed,
> We drowned a long La Bassée thirst—
> Trenches in June make throats damned dry.[1]

There were three rendezvous in Béthune which were especially patronized : the Pâtisserie, the Globe and the Red Lamp. Rendezvous, military generic term for meeting-place. Of these rendezvous the first two were variously favoured ; but since these establishments were used alone by Commissioned Officers, and the entertainment provided in them was wholly virtuous, even they were favoured equally according to the mood of the hour. The Prince patronized both, and, if for no other reason, so did we others. I always regretted that as the months passed by the Pâtisserie slowly garbed itself with the air and atmosphere of the " tea-shop," and for me it lost its charms.

[1] From " Corporal Stare," by Robert Graves.

In the earlier days when first we came to Béthune, late on Sunday morning following the hour of church, the Pâtisserie was filled with the quality of Béthune sipping coffee and sampling delicacies. We rubbed shoulders with them, choosing pastries and sweetmeats for immediate consumption, or to take back to the mess. And then we were part of France. In the back parlour of the shop were tables, much sought after, at which men could dally over steaming chocolate, and, in a pretence of disputing the modest charge, flirt with the young ladies who ministered to their needs. The Pâtisserie had no competitors, though there were other shops which dispensed teas and cakes. No maidens of Béthune were ever so beautiful as those of the Pâtisserie, and no tea, no coffee, no chocolate could be brewed with so rare a flavour as that prepared by their hands. The Pâtisserie remained unique. Veritably it was the Rumpelmayer of the Western Front.

The Globe possessed a speciality. Champagne. " Bubbly " of the best. Not the sweetly-flavoured vintages customary to France, but those reserved especially for England ; dry, crisp, sparkling gold. And it was cheap, miraculously cheap. For us in earlier years champagne had been reserved for a glass or two at Christmas ; or maybe surreptitiously filched from the tables of the elders at a children's party. But at the Globe this sparkling nectar ran almost like water, discharged from bottles from some fathomless cellar. Man could always find a friend in Béthune, for, standing in the street, the

Warrior from the line could look across the table-
tops, down the crowded length of the bar, twice
that of a cricket pitch, and search the laughing faces
hovering above the glasses. At the Globe were
manufactured far more stories than ever came out
of the Chelsea Arts Club or the Stock Exchange.
And I believe that birth was first here given to
much of that classic ribaldry attached to the names
of famous Generals.

" Begone dull care ! " The Globe, a half-bottle
of champagne, and the " strafes " of a commanding
officer or the enemy had burst with the bubbles ;
and all the weariness and disappointments of trench
warfare and raids were submerged in the glitter of
dancing eyes and scintillating wine.

But the Globe and the Pâtisserie were unofficial.
Their success relied upon the private enterprise of
both proprietor and customers. Not so Béthune's
third outstanding attraction—the Red Lamp. Such
patronage as this establishment secured—and it was
considerable—was largely that of curiosity. Indeed,
one may wonder if the Red Lamp was a necessary
contribution by officialdom to the amenities of
Béthune. The medical pundits, who set up and
ordained the house, seem to have paid little heed to
the psychological attitude of young men to such
matters.

Neither growing lads, scarcely out of their " teens,"
nor Englishmen unaccustomed to a feast prepared
in the manner of the eating-house, required such
relief or so unsavoury a presentation. If men sought
romance they found it. And its relish consisted in

the spice of adventure. The Red Lamp provided neither the dish nor the sauce. Psychologically it failed : and I doubt if it prevented a casualty from disease.

It is ridiculous to suppose that the abstinence of Adam from his Eve due to the semi-monastic seminary of a dug-out and the cloisters of the front and support lines could be compensated either by the routine of reliefs or by that of the Red Lamp. Man is not a donkey to be led forward by dangling a carrot in front of his nose.

Men were marvellously faithful to a wife or a sweetheart at home. They were incredibly loyal to one another. No paradox in that, no camouflage. The simple naked truth. Men cannot live even closer to each other than man and wife, week in week out, by day, by night, and hour by hour without sharing the closest confidence. Nor will they break faith. There will be no breach. Nor was there. From this sprang comradeship and *esprit de corps*.

If it is yet imagined that these men were guilty of sin against the moral code, expended their virtue in debauchery, then have a look round any city, provincial town or village throughout the length and breadth of the British Isles. As is man's behaviour, so it was in Flanders. Mostly good, some weak vessels, a few bad. Every police court knows its maintenance orders, every village its indiscretions. Human nature would be different otherwise.

In the early days of the British invasion of France, too, the inhabitants still welcomed the novelty of foreigners. Farmers and householders may have been resentful of the intrusion, but maidens and some wives whose young men and husbands, conscripts, had been summoned south, many already who had died *pour la patrie*, were in a mood to show more than hospitality to the invading legions of Britain's youth. History demonstrates that in war the birth-rate always rises. Objectively, this fact has no evil import for the race. On the contrary, for example, publicly and almost officially, an increase in the population of the Pas de Calais was welcomed by France. At this distance we can afford to smile, even as we laughed then, when we recall an illustration.

CHAPTER XVI

LOOS AND VIMY

A network of trenches—Customs—The first hundred thousand—Hill 60
—Cemeteries—The Canadian victory—Trenches—Retrospect.

In the spring of 1916 the area forward of Béthune
became a labyrinth of trenches, in which in earlier
days had fought the French and Germans and the
first British soldiers. Bits of Frenchmen, and hands
and feet of Germans, stuck grotesquely out of the
parapets and from tumbling trench sides. There
was a chaos of tins and rusty rifles of many patterns.
From the rat-chewed trousers covering a bleak
pelvis bone one could judge how suddenly the
French reserves had been called to war. These
trousers were red; and long blue overcoats, like
dressing-gowns, hung beside the collapsing dug-
outs, sometimes crowned with a *képi*.

It was in these festering ditches that the myriads
of rats which swarmed our neat trenches were
billeted and held their war councils. These rats
were as large as dogs; and in some cases became
almost domesticated, daily visitors, with pet nick-
names. But for the most part relentless war was
waged upon these loathsome intruders; and along
the parapets were arranged all kinds of cunning
traps, nooses and devices with which to snare them
to death. And in Béthune began the songs of the
War, which have now been carried to all quarters
of the earth. They are heard in the bazaars of
India, among the foothills of the Himalayas, in the
kraals of South Africa, on the Yang-tse, and are

chanted by nomads in the deserts of the Sudan. " Community singers " shout them uproariously, so that they have passed into the currency of every gathering of men. Soldiers liked the sentimental ones best; and they would sit in a disused factory rigged as a concert hall, in Béthune, pleasantly fumed by clouds of tobacco smoke, warmed by contact with hot humanity and perhaps a little addled after a visit to the Globe or to some other estaminet. And they would sing " Keep the home fires burning," and some lads going up to " The Brickstacks " or to the " Hohenzollern Redoubt " next day would hold hands and the lower lip would quiver while they sang " Roses are blooming in Picardy," and similar sentimental favourites.

Along the front line at intervals there would be hung brass shell-cases, empty, often polished, as a note of decoration to a well-swept trench, until some gust of shell-fire or gross bomb would spatter its mud walls with blood, and churn its footway with the pulp of flesh. These cases were used as gongs, to give the awful warning that a light breeze, coming as a benison to cool the midday heat, was green and foul and fœtid, laden with gas. The fumes, released from cylinders, would open like the petals of a flower, and then in wide ethereal fronds would be wafted towards the lines.

The little golden gongs, like the bells of a Burmese temple, would recall men from idle tasks to the disciplines, more binding than those of religion, and in an ecstasy of terror they would thrust their heads

into the masks which might save their souls.
" S.O.S. ! " Up went the signal in rocket flares ; and
the cry " Gas ! " echoed along the line. In British,
French and German trenches, this ritual was
observed ; and sometimes gas would be released
from cylinders, and at others in storms of shells,
which fell almost silently with a sibilant whisper
and a faint pop as they burst quietly and released
their fumes.

Hearken to how a poet of the War has described
the phenomenon of gas :

Bent double, like old beggars under sacks,
Knock-kneed, coughing like hags, we cursed through sludge,
Till on the haunting flares we turned our backs,
And towards our distant rest began to trudge.
Men marched asleep.   Many had lost their boots,
But limped on, blood-shod.   All went lame, all blind ;
Drunk with fatigue ; deaf even to the hoots
Of gas-shells dropping softly behind.

Gas !   Gas !   Quick, boys !—An ecstacy of fumbling,
Fitting the clumsy helmets just in time,
But someone still was yelling out and stumbling
And flound'ring like a man in fire or lime.
Dim through the misty panes and thick green light,
As under a green sea, I saw him drowning.

In all my dreams before my helpless sight,
He plunges at me, guttering, choking, drowning.

If in some smothering dreams you too could pace
Behind the waggon that we flung him in,
And watch the white eyes wilting in his face,
His hanging face, like a devil's sick of sin ;
If you could hear, at every jolt, the blood
Come gargling from the froth-corrupted lungs
Bitten as the cud
Of vile, incurable sores on innocent tongues,—

My friend, you would not tell with such high zest
To children ardent for some desperate glory,
The old Lie: *Dulce et decorum est*
Pro patria mori.[1]

The Prince of Wales was ubiquitous, turning up
in all kinds of astonishing places : " blowing " into
a dug-out for a drink, pacing about in most un-
pleasant places, " tin-hat " askew and smoking a
" gasper," making himself familiar with the lie of
the land, with men, and not least with the absurd
vocabulary.

No visitor of the War generation can enter
Béthune without feelings of sadness, which impression the bleak landscape only serves to heighten.
Béthune, filled with high hope and gaiety, witnessed
the destruction of the flower of Britain's youth.
The gallant new Divisions which marched to Loos
were decimated. Two Divisions of the First
Hundred Thousand remained but as fragments.
On the first day no less than 470 officers and 1,500
men fell, the attack being held at every point. On
the second day the losses were as heavy. One
Brigade sacrificed 78 officers and 2,000 men out of
the 3,600 who went to the attack. Of Battalions,
for example, the 8th West Kents lost their Colonel,
24 officers and 556 men ; and the 8th Buffs, their
Colonel, 24 officers and 534 men. The 15th Durham
Light Infantry lost their Colonel, 18 officers and
400 men.

The Guards Division which came to the support
of the new Battalions was half decimated, losing

---

[1] *Dulce et Decorum est*, Wilfred Owen.

3,000 men. Most of the young troops who went to the battle had never heard before the whine of a bullet: for two days they were cut off from all supplies of food and water, and were torn to pieces. The 15th Scottish Division became the focus of the attack; and the line of their corpses marked the farthest point of advance. To such futility did a gallant piper march up and down on the parapet under heavy fire, warming the blood of crouching men with the maddening skirl of his pipes. Three British Divisional Commanders were killed during the battle. The left flank of the attack was the "Hohenzollern Redoubt," where another new Scottish Division, the 9th, made its attack opposite the village of Haisnes. "Fosse Eight" lay just to the left of this stronghold.

For the first time on September 25th, 1915, gas cylinders were employed by the British, no less than 5,000 being dug into the front parapet, but an unfortunate breeze blew the fumes back upon the attack. Within a few moments of Zero Hour the quarries and slag heaps ran red with blood; and even a serious historian, but one who did his best to see the conduct of British Armies through rose-hued spectacles, relates that "the ardent soldiers dashed forward upon their desperate venture." [1] In one Battalion, the 6th King's Own Scottish Borderers, 19 officers led the men over the parapet, and within a few moments the whole 19, including the Colonel and Second-in-Command, lay dead or wounded upon the ground; while 500 men had

[1] *British Campaigns in Europe*, by Conan Doyle.

IN THE STEPS OF
ST. PAUL

H. V. Morton's new book will command attention throughout the world as the account of a modern traveller following the missionary journeys of St. Paul, thus tracing the route by which Christianity came to the West.

The author's intention is to show St. Paul as the saint and as the man, to indicate the problems which faced him when he set out to Christianise the pagan world, to describe the world in which he lived, and to contrast the cities of that world with their condition to-day, as revealed to a modern traveller.

In order to do this, he has made four journeys to the Near East during the past two years. The territory he has covered includes Palestine, Syria, Turkey, Macedonia, Greece, Cyprus, Malta and Rhodes. Among the cities associated with St. Paul which Mr. Morton describes are Tarsus, Jerusalem, Antioch, Salonika, Athens and Rome. His wanderings have taken him to the ruined cities of Salamis and Paphos in Cyprus, Ephesus, Iconium, Lystra and Derbe in Asia Minor, Philippi and Beroea in Macedonia, and Corinth in Greece.

Mr. Morton took the Four Gospels as his guide to Palestine when he was writing " IN THE STEPS OF THE MASTER." In the Near East he has been guided by the Epistles of St. Paul and the Acts of the Apostles.

We are convinced that this book will command a greater public than any other contribution to Pauline literature. An entirely new vigour and interest are imparted to the subject by the personal observation which illuminates the book. The 300,000 readers of " IN THE STEPS OF THE MASTER " will find in this new book the same blend of biblical commentary and fine descriptive writing.

7s. 6d.	20s.	£5 5 0
32 pages of Illustrations	64 pages of Illustrations	Limited Edition

ORDER FORM

To .... (Booksellers)

Please supply the following books published
by Rich & Cowan:

Number	Title	Price
....	....	....
....	....	....
....	....	....
....	....	....
....	....	....
....	....	....
....	....	....
....	....	....
....	....	....

£   :   :

IN THE STEPS OF
THE MASTER

His reverence and affection for the country never falter . . .
The book bears marks of the trouble that has gone to its
making in its freedom from mistakes . . . a book that is sure
to win wide popularity. *THE OBSERVER*

He is in his element—observant, enthusiastic, chivalrous and
the best of company. *PUNCH*

This is easily the best descriptive book on Palestine that has
appeared in recent years. Mr. Morton has a rare gift of
seizing the truly significant feature, not only of an ancient
landscape but in the life of a people. He is reverent in the
presence of what is worthy of reverence, considerate of the
feelings of others in relation to sacred things, and possessed
of an equipment of historic knowledge and insight that make
his book a real contribution to an already great and growing
literature . . . To a degree that is quite exceptional Mr.
Morton has managed to enter into the abiding spirit of the
tiny country that is venerated as the home of the three most
powerful faiths in the world.
CHURCH OF ENGLAND NEWSPAPER

The spirit of this pilgrim-guide is at once sympathetic, reverent
and intensely alive, so that the book he has given us is not
only of high value to all visiting the Holy Land, but in its
vividness is excellent and often edifying reading to the many
who cannot make the pilgrimage . . . Mr. Morton is not a
Catholic, but he has a profound and vital sense of the truth
and beauty contained in the Faith. The illustrations are well
chosen and admirably reproduced.
CATHOLIC HERALD

To travel in his company is a singularly moving and enriching
experience . . . he is so consistently interesting that it is
impossible to skip a line of his narrative . . . the most fasci-
nating travel book any visitor to Palestine has ever written,
and one of the most revealing commentaries on Holy Writ.
It is a book to read and re-read . . . not only Mr. Morton's
best book yet, but, for the student of the Gospels and their
country, the best book of the season.
METHODIST RECORDER

7s. 6d.   20s.   £5 5s. 0d.

PUBLISHED BY

RICH & COWAN, LTD.

25 SOHO SQUARE, W.1

been cut down as with a scythe in the long grass which faced the German trenches. The 11th Durham Light Infantry lost 10 officers and 500 men in the first rush; while wounded and unwounded alike suffered untold agonies from the gas which hung thickly about the British trenches. Along the whole front of the attack was shown incredible valour but the carnage was hideous.

The new and untried Divisions were brought into battle after three long night marches, made longer by the constant traffic blocks of the road. They reached the attack positions without food and none overtook them. They had no clear-cut orders as to their objectives. The skies poured with intermittent showers. Before they ever reached the battle, these superb troops were not only tired and hungry but soaked to the skin; and before they were launched to the attack, throughout the night they had been pelted with bombs from in front, their communications had been shattered behind, and their prospects were as black and starless as the sky above them.

Loos remains hideous in history, with its trivial gains; and the important towns of La Bassée and Lens rested always in the hands of the enemy, and were held by them until they withdrew quietly in August, 1918.

In this area lies also the battlefield of Neuve Chapelle of March, 1915, and of Hill 60.

No contrast could surely be greater than that between the Oriental pageantry of India and the cold, sordid trench lines of Neuve Chapelle. In thinking of India, inevitably there are conjured to the mind the princely splendours of Maharajahs, dazzling light, deep shadows, a kaleidoscope of colour. The thronged bazaars hum with the tumult of many tongues and cries, the temple bells recite the weird discord of mystic melody. The *muezzin* calls the faithful as the last light flickers behind the shadowed palms. The *Sadhu* murmurs prayers beside the lotus pool. Perfumes besiege the senses, musk and incense ; ox-drawn waggons creak to eternity along the dusty roads. The crowds, festooned with saffron, vermilion, magenta, the ends of their *phetas* waving like pennants in the breeze, dance to the cymbal and the drum.

But in Flanders all was changed. No *djinn* of night might ever present the terrors of the trenches between Festubert and Armentières : no kind of *Kale* conceived the carnage of Neuve Chapelle.

The sound of men's feet pacing in unison brought the people to their doors ; and they were brown men whom they saw—wild-looking Baluchies, handsome Pathans, yelling drabies and syces ; horsemen from the Punjab armed with quivering lances, stocky Gurkhas from far Nepal in the Himalayas. The Pathan roams the mountains, rifle in hand, to pursue a blood feud, in search of his quarry. But on the flats of Neuve Chapelle his foe was unseen and unknown. His legs were caught up in coils of barbed wire, and he perished in a storm of shells and bombs. The loss in British officers was extraordinarily high. Flanders was no battle-ground for

Indians; yet the contribution of India filled a vital breach.

There are some forty cemeteries east of Béthune; and the Memorials to the 46th and 55th Divisions are here established. But most of those who died at Loos remained, as did those who fell in the ravine before Gommecourt, lying in No-Man's-Land, caught up in the barbed wire, and strewn upon the blackened excrescences. Loos was a foretaste of the Somme, very bitter.

Go south from this stricken area to its topographical limit, and stand on Vimy Ridge, with its wide view over Artois and Arras. Vimy played its part in April, 1917, as the left wing of the Battle of Arras. Whatever may be said concerning the main battle in this war of attrition, the attack of Vimy was a conspicuous success, with which the name of Canada will always be associated. The Canadian National Memorial stands high on the ridge amid the Canadian cemeteries; and there are other Memorials to the 1st Canadian Division and to the Canadian Artillery. Béthune is but twelve miles from Vimy, and here the mining area ends, giving way to the ploughed fields and root crops which are the character of all the country between Arras and the Somme. One has to go farther east again to find the mines; and among them, but with far less bloodshed, the British troops fought at Mons and Valenciennes.

.   .   .   .   .   .

Away over the fields of Flanders and Picardy, rolling downs or great flats under root crops, the

s

Pilgrim will always find remains from the scrap-heap of War. It may be from a hedgerow that the nozzle of a shell protrudes, or lying in a ditch there are shreds of equipment. A steel helmet serves to hold grain for the chickens of a cottager; and stumps of trees are pitted with rusting metal. Some places, marked by the hand of war, will never lose the changes wrought upon them. They have been so deeply dug, so grossly shattered and exploded.

There is no area of the battlefields which is not somewhere thus marked for all time. Sometimes these places have been preserved, as at Hill 60 and in Gommecourt Park; but in others the confusion remains, copses pulped with barbed wire, and the chalk downs upheaved beyond human aid, as at High Wood and Croisilles. The traveller off the beaten track will come suddenly upon such remains. He may find a chalk quarry in which, as they were, lie ammunition boxes and metal clips yet filled with ammunition. There will be tins, empty, the remains of a last meal, a rusted bayonet which served as a toasting-fork, and probably a boot, to show that this was man's habitation. And the woods, though carefully searched and combed for human remains, yet yield the sight of a bone, and rifle barrels protrude from among the roots and undergrowth. In woods, such as those of Mametz and High Wood, so staunched with blood, the wild blackberries grow as large as plums amid a chaos of pits, shell-made and dug, which time may never efface.

In the former trenches, which, here and there,

the traveller may visit, he can experience something of the life of the warrior. He must stoop as
he goes, taking care lest his head be seen above the
parapet. He must be ready to dive into a dug-out
to escape a shell storm, unless he be the sentry
with eyes piercing a loophole, when he must cling
to the shaking parapet and hope for the best. Or,
he may imagine that he is one of attack or counter-
attack. With bomb, bludgeon or pistol in hand, he
must run from one traverse to another, bobbing,
stumbling over corpses, leaping across upturned
timbers, treading upon broken humanity as he
surges down the trench. The shell-case, hanging
as an alarm gong in the parapet, will be beaten;
and, no matter what he is doing, he will seize his
gas mask and fasten it over his head. Then he
will mount the firing-step, peering through goggles
across No-Man's-Land. He will imagine the earth
being upheaved to his front, covered by wisps of
white or green smoke, eddying towards him; and
through the mists he will see the phantom shapes
of armed men bearing down upon him. He will
hear cries of alarm and agony from either side.
And, as he peers along the sights of machine gun
or rifle, he will observe those hurrying figures to the
front suddenly throw their arms in the air and
pitch face-forwards, or spin and fall and writhe before
his eyes. The attack may have been successful,
and, if so, he must stand with his hands in the air,
defeated, a prisoner, while grimed men, speaking a
foreign tongue, hurry past him, until he must leave
the shattered trench and the broken bodies of his

comrades and march east or west to be placed behind a screen of barbed wire.

The attack may have been beaten off; and as the drum-fire wilts and dies, he will stand down for respite, to clean first his arms, and then to inquire who among his comrades of an hour earlier yet remain alive. The trench-walls will be spattered with blood; there will be moans of agony; and men bearing stretchers will be lifting and carrying the wounded and separating them from the dead. An officer re-orders the defence: the trench must be repaired; and the routine of four years begins again from where it was suddenly checked. The ration parties, carrying sand-bags, move along the trench; a postman distributes letters and newspapers. A General, with his Staff inspects. Digging, endless digging, to fashion new posts and communication ways, becomes the order of the day. A mouth-organ or a chanter, even a wheezing gramophone from the depths of a dug-out, make their music heard. The sergeant-major has his little say; and without it trench life would be different. As dusk descends, there will be movement. Parties carrying rolls of wire prepare to mount the parapet and to go into No-Man's-Land to strengthen the defence of obstacles. A trench raid may be mustered, armed with bombs, ready, under cover of darkness, to rush the intervening space between friend and enemy, to destroy a machine-gun nest or to bring back a prisoner for identification that the movements of the enemy may be known.

But whatever he is doing, let the visitor to the

trenches " keep his head down." Criss-crossing every trench were telephone wires, balks of timber to provide cover, and over the communication ways ran the light railways upon which material and munitions were brought up by night to the front lines. Every man must bend as he hurries, and hurry he must, along a trench; and he must bend even lower as he enters one of the shafts which led into the bowels of the earth, where in some kind of safety men ate and slept, cursed and jested, and wrote their letters home. The traveller may stand in some famous wood and re-experience the fear with which ever tree was invested. Behind their trunks a sniper stood: hid among their leafy branches, a sharp-shooter watched for the enemy. Dug in amid the undergrowth were subterranean ways from which armed men would leap to the front, in the back and on either side. These woods were fearful.

There is scarcely a hedge or ditch within the battle zone which has not some tale to tell; and often the remains of ammunition and equipment, scarcely covered by dust and peeping from the tufted grass, will yield to the imagination a story of heroism and of sacrifice. And in the new-built villages the mind can readily re-summon marching men and idlers, clothed in khaki, sky-blue or grey, men of hearts and ideals, made from a common clay, part of the universal mind of the universe, who from the bitterness of war have discovered a new comradeship from which is being born a common objective for the human family.

INDEX

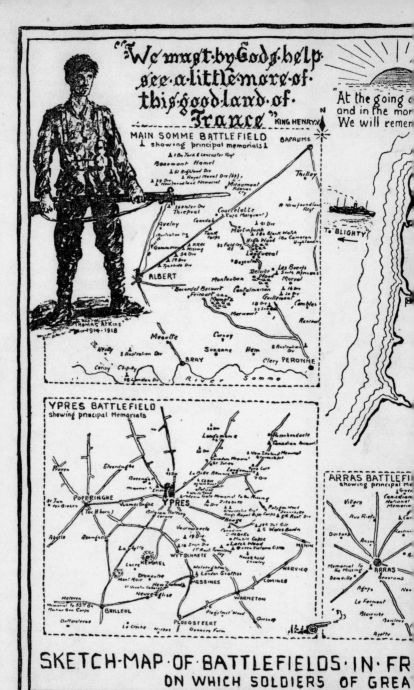